THE REAL ECONOMY

DR. FRED BLANCHARD

outskirtspress
DENVER, COLORADO

The opinions expressed in this manuscript are solely the opinions of the author and do not represent the opinions or thoughts of the publisher. The author has represented and warranted full ownership and/or legal right to publish all the materials in this book.

The Real Economy
All Rights Reserved.
Copyright © 2016 Dr. Fred Blanchard
v3.0

Cover Photo © 2016 Dr. Fred Blanchard. All rights reserved - used with permission.

This book may not be reproduced, transmitted, or stored in whole or in part by any means, including graphic, electronic, or mechanical without the express written consent of the publisher except in the case of brief quotations embodied in critical articles and reviews.

Outskirts Press, Inc.
http://www.outskirtspress.com

ISBN: 978-1-4787-7474-7

Outskirts Press and the "OP" logo are trademarks belonging to Outskirts Press, Inc.

PRINTED IN THE UNITED STATES OF AMERICA

TABLE OF CONTENTS

Abstract i

Preface iii

1. The Theory of Two 1
2. Proxies as Exchange 17
3. Two Economies One Means of Exchange 28
4. The Economic History of the United States 41
5. The kcal Economy 51
6. The Real Economy 54
7. Inflation 98
8. The Fuel Consumption Equation 100
9. The Demise of the Dinosaurs 102
10. Restoring the American Dream 104
11. Power to the People 108
12. Implementing the Impossible 111
13. The Final Arbitrage 114
14. The Ultimate Result 117

ABSTRACT

It is the objective of this essay to prove that all governments constituted to date have purposely misused their power by first adopting a false proxy for their economies and then skewing its distribution in favor of those who have allowed them to maintain that power. The consequence of this misuse is the ultimate consumption of the earth's resources and the starvation of its population. This conclusion is inevitable in any case because the earth's resources are finite, a kcal measured economy is proposed that will prolong it almost indefinitely. It will more equally share nature's bounty and reward those who contribute more than their share. The sanctity of the family is the only thing that will enable the survival of the human race and only the economic system described in this paper can insure it. Its implementation and success requires only one caveat "thou shalt not steal".

You have often heard the expression, "money doesn't grow on trees". I hate to disappoint you but this statement is false. Not only does it grow on trees but, on bushes and in the earth. It is the food that provides life and the ability to produce work. Ignorance of that fact has resulted in two economies, a life economy and a style economy. The fact that the second has dwarfed the first has caused us to lose sight of the fact that it is the first that enables and drives the second. Further clouding the source of our real economy has been man's ingenuity in enhancing nature through an increasing ability to obtain higher and higher yields of nature's reproducible assets. Our euphoria over the ability to continue to enhance our style of life has resulted in ignoring the reality that the earth's resources, in particular its land and water are not limitless.

God was right when he set down to Moses the only law necessary for man's survival and that is "thou shalt not steal". The punishment for doing so was reserved to God in the hereafter. When God discovered that Adam and Eve could not govern themselves and stole His apple He banished them from the Garden. Then man, in his inimitable attempt to play God on earth, established government to enforce the law and punish lawbreakers but in the process gave it the power to distribute nature's wealth unevenly to those who then owned it.

Every government established since the adoption of paper money or non-reproducible proxies as a substitute for the fuel value of food that enables the economy to run contain a fatal flaw that has caused governments to fail. This paper exposes that flaw and provides a proof that all of the governments that have overlooked this flaw have or will ultimately fail. Events in Africa and the Middle East give proof it is already occurring on a grand scale as nature's renewable assets are stretched beyond limits. Fortunately it is not too late for the United States, as almost the last bastion of nature's surplus, to adopt an alternative economic system. That system will not eliminate the inevitable when water or the nutrients necessary to replace those used in the process of photosynthesis run out but the one described will extend human life far longer.

This paper first posits the true measure of man and his relationship among others in an economic system is the fuel of life. It exposes the folly of a metal proxy for exchange. It then explains why paper currency cannot serve as a proxy for metal and why it must be supported by means of the fuel that provides life. Then it explains how our economic system is failing and why. All is not yet lost because the real economy can still be implemented and its workings explained in some detail. Explaining the follies of those who have manipulated the economic system shows how difficult it has been to replace a system that has been in use for literally thousands of years and why it may no longer be possible to reverse or forestall man's ultimate demise.

PREFACE

We live in an age where the skeptics claim we are losing the ability to achieve the "American Dream". Before one can lose something it had to first be obtained but, what exactly is it? Is it getting married, settling down and raising a family? If it is, you had better have and be close to parents or grandparents who will take care of your children while both you and your wife work to make ends meet. Is it self-sufficiency? If that is what it is, one cannot attain it on their own because they must first survive youth and learn the wherewithal to be able to be self-sufficient and having learned it from others there must be a job available to which to apply that knowledge. A bear cub, having been taught to forage for food faces the ultimate dilemma when there is none or what is available is desired by another. Is it being whatever one wants to be? If you are satisfied with self-teaching and have the financial independence to survive you are indeed fortunate. If not you will require someone to teach you and further the opportunity offered by society to compete against others with similar skills in order to earn a living. If none of the above you will have to resort to a plan B.

This paper to demonstrates that whatever way you define the "American Dream" we never fully achieved it nor would we under the system devised by the framers of our constitutions. The reason is it contained a fatal flaw carried over from its English predecessor in that it allowed some to exercise the only right prohibited by God, the right to steal.

Man has evolved well beyond the point of mere survival. Had it not been for his ability to first adapt to what nature provided but to magnify and modify nature itself he would have multiplied beyond what nature alone could support. A theory of what happened to the dinosaurs and other species is given in Chapter 9. When man no longer became dependent on what nature supplied but on other men the economy changed from one of sharing to ownership and those who owned natures supply made the rules for its distribution. They not only made the rules for the economy in their favor, but chose the wrong medium as well.

Webster defines economy as the management of the income and expenditures of a family, private business or government. When there were only families its economy's income was the gathering and preparation of food and securing shelter and clothing each of which was shared on the basis of need. In exchange the parents spent their time on the basis of ability. A family could survive if it could protect itself and reproduce enabling its older members to survive when they could no longer produce. No money or exchange was needed and the only thing one owned were what one could make and carry with them. Families soon morphed into tribes because man had no natural enemies he couldn't vanquish, outside himself, and the elders of the families saw to it that all the members of the tribes shared not only income but expenditure of their time to produce that income. Tribal leaders also meted out punishment to those who took from others what did not belong to them. The basis of life was the fuel value of food and the only law to insure it was "thou shalt not steal".

In his evolution man soon learned to fashion tools that reduced the time it took to secure and process his food and to enhance the production of nature through the cultivation of grains, vegetables, fruits and even animals. The consequence was man no longer had to be a nomad, he could settle down in one place and his food would come to him if he or someone else went and got it.   At least it would come to a market where he could barter what he could make in excess to his own needs for that which he didn't have, the first barter being that for food and thereafter clothing and shelter which he would consume over a longer period of time before needing or wanting replacements.

A second economy was developing, the first being the one that insured survival. The second economy I shall call the "style economy" and the first the "life economy". Together they complete the lifestyle that each of us enjoys and uses to compare one to another. The only condition required for these economies to exist was the land being occupied by the population had to produce the food necessary for its survival.

Nature alone once determined if man would survive by providing the food and man the means to obtain it. Only man's ingenuity to supplement nature has enabled his growing numbers to avoid extinction to where his very survival is now totally dependent on his supplement of nature. Sharing has evolved into trade and the only thing that man has to trade is time. That time is made available in the form of work and is enabled by the consumption of fuel.

A family, a tribe, even a country is a closed society, its only commonality the language by which its citizens communicate and the economic system by which they survive and prosper. Its very existence depends on having enough food on which to survive. Its ability to prosper depends on how the society's members use their time in interactions with each other in trade for the fruits of their labor. The later requires a measure of equity if exchanges are to be made on some basis other than charity. Like the game of Monopoly, where each player is given his stake to start, in the game of life the measure you need to survive and have the hours available to exchange must be delivered to all citizens equally on the basis of the amount that nature makes available during each growing cycle. It acknowledges the fact that your share is available and you may save it or spend it to obtain first food and then on whatever embellishments others have made available and you can afford.

I submit that in a barter economy that unconsciously those making trades make assumptions on the basis of how long it would take to produce the product or service if one had the skill and the time to do so. It is an example of free trade the common measure being that of time. If one has nothing tangible to trade but their time there must be some proxy that represents, at a minimum, the food (fuel) necessary for survival that one must have in order to produce the hours required to earn a living.

In order for a proxy to represent the value of food it must have two characteristics; it must be reproducible and consumable by the individual. It must also have a constant measure because the characteristics of what it represents as a proxy does not change and that is the kilocalorie (kcal) that is the measure of the fuel value of food.

1

THE THEORY OF TWO

The Theory

The human body is an engine. It consumes fuel in the form of food and produces the energy that is used to fuel the functions of the body for survival and to produce work. Like most engines the human body is composed of parts capable of burning fuel at different rates in order to produce varying degrees of power. Like any other engine its design has both an upper and lower limit. The lower limit is the fuel necessary to keep the engine running and the upper limit is the amount of fuel that can be converted to produce the maximum conversion of fuel to physical energy. It is the intent of this chapter to prove that the maximum sustainable output is twice the lower limit.

The Proof

The vital parts of the body are designed to operate, that is convert fuel to energy, in a range of minimum to maximum. Some parts are provided in pairs to facilitate the total function and improve efficiency. These are the arms, the legs, the eyes, ears, lungs and kidneys. The muscles, including the heart and the brain, are energy consumers. The loss of one, where there are initially two, does not affect the capacity of the human body to survive, only the ability to maximize its output. It is estimated that when operating normally, the human body consumes between 2000 kilocalories (kcal) and 3000 kcal per day depending on

THE REAL ECONOMY

the size of the body. Initially most of the kcals are consumed in building the body to its maximum size and in later life to maintaining bodily function. Based on physical activity level (PAL) and the body mass ratio (BMR) the United Nations Food and Agriculture Organization has determined the average population's kcal consumption to be within the range indicated. It is estimated the average human body can produce about 0.1 horsepower indefinitely. One horsepower is equivalent to ten kcal per minute. Therefore 0.1 horsepower equals 1 kcal/min. There are 1440 minutes in 24 hours and if the body consumes between 2000 kcal and 3000 kcal per day in fuel and can produce about 1440 kcal in output it is not unreasonable to assume that the body, acting as a machine is approximately 50% efficient. That is, it can convert about half the energy contained in its fuel to useful energy.

Food is the fuel necessary to sustain life and the energy in that fuel is measured in kcal. Barter and coinage no longer suffice as means of exchange or proxy for food that is the primary purchase for consumption. Paper currency serves this function so long as it has the characteristics of what it serves as proxy and that is being reproducible and its measure equated to the kcal. Gold, or any other non-reproducible commodity will not suffice for the simple reason it is limited in availability and its relationship to the kcal is variable since its production requires variable amounts of kcal. The U. S. Dollar does not suffice for this purpose because it too has no constant measure to support it and is constantly being diluted by borrowing. It is indirectly backed by the kcal because the United States still produces more kcal than necessary to sustain the population but requires subsidies in order to maintain this surplus and distributes much of it in welfare to those who have no work. Time and the continuing increase in population without commensurate food production will ultimately result first in rationing and then abandonment as a new government is constituted to repeat the process again.

The fuel requirements to perform normal human tasks are more easily

THE THEORY OF TWO

ascertained than that of determining the value of acquiring the skill to perform all functions yourself. I would posit however, that if you believe it would take you more than twice as long you are better off paying to have it done by someone skilled and practiced at the task. The condition being that the pay is measured in the kcal necessary to produce work.

Rather than intuit this from a zero start it is more efficient to start from what we know and work backwards to see if there is some logical path in order to reach that reality, a process called reverse engineering. We all know that some people are all thumbs and cannot get the grasp of things no matter how they try and there are those who by their nature pick up things rapidly. These are the exceptions rather than the rule and the body's central processing unit, the brain, as the controller of all of the body's functions is instinctively preprogramed to perform the minimum functions necessary for survival and these are the processing of fuel to produce the energy for survival and that to produce useful work.

If you are alive, nature has already given you the time to perform the necessary tasks to sustain and enhance life. Until the availability of artificial light you had approximately half the day to perform these tasks and the other half to rest. With the advent of the family came the division of labor and more efficient use of time but increased the dependence on others to either help or perform the various functions for both survival and to produce the things that enhanced the style of life. Commensurate with this growth in numbers were the development of new groupings and the delineation of territory, accompanied by commensurate increases in agricultural production that is now cultivated instead of naturally occurring. Skills which were once developed for only temporary or intermittent uses became occupations whose acquisition enabled its owners to sell their time for that of others including the farmers, processors and distributors of food to complete the life cycle.

THE REAL ECONOMY

There are two forms of labor; the mental part that is thinking about how a thing is to be done and the physical act of doing it. Performing something for the first time is as if something has never been done before and one must simulate mentally the various ways it can be done and selecting from the developed alternatives, usually the one which requires the least physical movements to conserve energy (fuel). The second is to watch it being performed and then emulate it. A third is to read and follow a written instruction. A fourth is to hear it performed, like a song and be able to reproduce it by humming, singing or whistling it. The highest form of the latter is to be able to reproduce it on a musical instrument.

If we could program the brain to intuitively perform certain functions through practice and repetition and learn the shortcuts to minimize the time necessary one can then perform them more rapidly than one who must take the time to think about them and then repeat them physically. It stands to reason then if the time for the brain to have to think through the physical process could be reduced to zero the time that can be achieved in executing the physical process would be halved. The amount of fuel consumed in the process would also be halved. This would be impossible because the brain must still take the time to execute the preprogrammed activity.

Nearly everyone confuses facilitation with supervision. A person who has been trained in a task needs no supervision, only facilitation to be able to execute it. If you work for yourself you need no supervision but you must perform all of the tasks associated with the time you are spending. The first is selling, the second is gathering the raw materials or wherewithal to execute the task, the third is performing the task and the last is delivering the goods. The most important is the execution because it requires the greatest skill and produces the results desired.

It has been posited that if you can perform a task yourself in twice the time as a professional who performs that task on a regular basis you

THE THEORY OF TWO

should opt to do it yourself. The reasoning being that you neither have the time nor desire to learn how to do it yourself or have the exchange (fuel equivalent surplus to your own needs). Conversely, if you can acquire a skill that enables you to perform a task in half the time of another unskilled person the opportunities arise that you can sell your time to those who want or need it and cannot perform it or it would take them more than twice the time.

The foregoing demonstrates that maximum utility is achieved under conditions of self-sufficiency but this condition cannot exist because at least two people must remain to insure the continuation of the species and when the numbers increase the complications of distance from the food source and the fact that many are incapable of self-sufficiency either temporarily or permanently to perform the necessary work to sustain life. This provides the opportunity for those who choose to work will be given the chance to obtain additional kcal by selling their time to those who need or want it. It also posits that the maximum one can demand for his time in a competitive environment is the hourly value of a distribution of nature's fuel as represented by an acceptable proxy, since less would be asked by someone unemployed or the individual will chose either to do it themselves or do without. There is also only a finite amount provided each growing season and is consumed or goes to waste. Earth's non-reproducible assets can accumulate but depreciate with time.

A typical example is that of cutting hair. You cannot do it yourself except for the excessive time it takes to do the same job as a professional barber. In a family a wife can cut the hair of her husband and children and save the cost of paying a professional. If she or her husband can sell their time for half or less than they would have to pay a Barber she and the Barber come out ahead. At worst the cost would be absorbed in discretionary income or the do without alternative employed. Under the rules of this form of economy monopolies are possible, but not likely and if they should occur, charging more than the last price for the good or service is considered theft and any unlawful gain taxed away.

Nature alone cannot produce the necessary kcal to feed the world's growing population and man has stepped in and enhanced nature such that with some exceptions sufficient food is available either through indigenous sources or trade. Enhancements in agriculture in addition to irrigation and fertilizers have maximized the output per crop acre. The most efficient crops that provide not only fuel but proteins and minerals necessary to sustain life are grains. If nothing else is grown they alone could support the highest population that could be sustained, all others mere embellishments. If world population stabilized where land and water were still in surplus other crops could be grown to vary the diet and kcal sources to enhance life's choices.

If man is considered as an engine his efficiency and output could be measured and his output compared with others. To be comparable there must be a measure that is a constant and it has been posited that is the kcal and the physical output between individuals has shown that training, whereby the physical actions can be made more efficient to the extent of nearly doubling the output through training and repetition that enables nearly double the physical production without increasing the fuel consumption. What about output that is nearly all mental and requires little or no physical effort other than speaking? Can you be trained so that you can nearly double or in this case halve the time it takes to perform the same task?

To answer these questions one must first acknowledge that the only naturally instinctive drive the human body possesses is to obtain fuel for survival. Without it the body will die and if a baby is abandoned by its mother and denied food the timing of the demise is a matter of hours and if denied water fewer hours still because water is necessary to process and distribute what energy is available in the form of food. Without oxygen, the time is reduced to minutes.

THE THEORY OF TWO

A newborn child knows neither day nor night only hunger requiring fuel and fatigue requiring rest. The human body is a constantly operating mechanism and totally undisciplined as to when to eat and sleep and yet it is born into an environment whose disciplinarian is the clock. The baby must be quickly trained into the adult routine or the parents make adjustments to adapt to the babies needs and put up with consequences of denying the training the absence of which commence at day one with signals from the child of the desire for fuel. We take no notice of the rest time because it is quiet and the demands for fuel suppressed. The use of pacifiers such as plastic nipples and the substitution of formula for mother's milk are part of the training the consequences of which are speculative but I think sufficient to demonstrate that with the exception of the need for fuel instinctive actions are the result of experience and training and not part of preprogramming of the core processing unit (CPU), the brain.

Communication is the expression of mental activity. When we want a baby to be quiet you will get no results by shouting "stop crying". The baby has not yet learned the word nor recognizes what it is you are telling them other than making noise. Immediate physical contact usually indicates to the baby that something that they are crying for is coming. When the results are forthcoming you provide a reward such as a feeding but, the training does not stop there. If the baby is not taught that they will not get a reward every time they start crying they will never stop. The reward to you is the spoiled child that usually turns into a spoiled adult. If something so fundamental and necessary is a learned behavior how can one but surmise that communicating one's thoughts and ideas are learned behaviors and do not become instinctive until practiced and continuously repeated. The proof is that until we communicate in a language with common understandings we do not know what the other person is talking about, writing or picturing.

We communicate in many ways. We use body language, both subtle and expressively overt. We draw pictures, using bold colors or black or white to provide nuance or emphasis. We speak using inflection and volume to convey importance or emphasis. We write, using words and put them in an orderly fashion to convey their meaning in a context. For example the words; wet, black, the, has, dog and nose are pure gibberish taken alone but fashioned into a sentence take on meaning such as; the black dog has a wet nose but, is that what we mean or, is it the wet dog has a black nose? It is a reminder that verbal communication is the most fallible. Just remember the story that is passed down a line of people until what comes out at the end often bears no resemblance to the story that started.

It is a given that our reading vocabulary is the best of the three we possess and they are reading, writing and finally verbal. When we read we understand well the words with which we are familiar and those we don't we can usually judge the meaning of from the context in which they are used. Many of us will consult a dictionary to be sure and when we do we usually remember the word and often add it to our own vocabulary, building a better understanding and a way to better express ourselves. We will not however read very much from authors who try to impress us with the breadth of their vocabulary nor will we pay much attention to people who speak a language we don't understand or use words we don't understand. It is said that Winston Churchill had the command of over 20,000 words in the English language. The average college graduate has a vocabulary between 6000 and 10,000 and the high school graduate about 4000 to 6000. It would be foolhardy for Churchill to try and impress people with his message using the breadth of his vocabulary because even if he had a message of very great import, he would have a small audience indeed of people who would understand him.

Rudolph Flesch developed tests that establishes a grade level standard for reading material that uses syllables and sentence length to determine the grade level at which a person should be able to comprehend what is written. It is mandated by law in many states to force insurance companies and lawyers to produce documents that the average person can comprehend. It was also a common adjunct to computer word processing programs but has since become optional because it was deemed discriminatory. It would seem reasonable that such a test could be employed in reverse to determine the comprehension level of individuals from work they compose. In any event, it is apparent that comprehension is the ability to put together or understand words whose meanings and contexts are understood by others of equal or greater comprehension. It would do well to remember this objective in deciding whether and what should be taught in government mandated public schools and how its results can be measured.

Like physical attributes, the speed at which one can assemble the words to communicate information can be nearly doubled if there is no need to think about them because they have been preassembled instinctively through practice and repetition. The practicality of this improvement is necessary only in the competitive environment of employment and should come after one learns how to ask for what one needs or wants, knows the difference between right and wrong and understands that interactions with others introduces responsibilities, obligations and accountability. Associated with these are rewards and punishments which form the foundation of the training that is to follow initial employment.

Whether in medicine, law, carpentry, plumbing or merely driving a truck or operating machinery the next step in life is employment in whatever area you have chosen or is available to you through the acquisition of the basic building blocks and your ability to take instruction. That will be instruction in acquisition and use of words and actions you have only been casually introduced to, read or heard about and are the specific language of the trade or profession. How rapidly you learn and can assimilate these words so that their use becomes instinctive will determine how rapidly you reach the compensation paid to the average performing worker the cost of which must be recovered from the customer by the business owner.

THE REAL ECONOMY

A man alone, in order to survive must be both a consumer and a producer. The body is in a constant state of processing the fuel provided by nature and its consumer has approximately 12 hours in which to gather at least the 2000 to 3000 kcal to supply it. How much of that time is actually consumed depends on the availability of the fuel and its concentration in the form of kcal per unit of weight. Grains have the highest concentration of kcal per unit weight. Rice, wheat and corn are among the most heavily cultivated but the preference is for wheat and rice for human consumption, corn being used primarily for animal feed. Wheat is probably the natural preference for the production of kcal as it requires the least amount of water of the three.

We have long since passed the ability of nature to produce sufficient food to feed the growing world population and were it not for improvements in crop production and natural loss due to genetic modification of seed the current population could not be supported and in some places is already deficient. The question is, if there is enough food being produced by the producers why must some do without and others consume more than they need? The answer is tied to that of another question and that is why are we forced to produce in order to consume?

When a man or woman marries they do so in recognition that two can live more cheaply than one alone. If the intent is also to create progeny they do so in recognition they will also have to assume their production will be adequate to provide for their offspring during their time of development to be producers. It is also in hopes that in exchange their progeny will be sufficiently productive to take care of them when they themselves become only consumers and in the event they have insufficient reserves to see to themselves. The family system works fine when the family shares because the ultimate survival of all is a dependency of one on the other. When one steals from another the system breaks down unless it is brought back into control. Control can be accomplished by only two alternatives; punishment sufficient to deter the thief from repeating their thievery or expulsion from the family.

As the numbers of people expand two things happen; more fuel must be produced and the labor required producing and delivering it increases but disproportionately. At its most efficient the additional labor required is 50%.

It has been shown that survival can be accomplished in three ways. You can earn it by performing all of the acts necessary to cultivate, harvest, process and distribute the fuel you require. You can share it with those who have a surplus or, you can steal it from them. It has been shown that in human development there are times, such as in infancy and in old age or because of some physical or mental impairment you are unable to work or the work is assigned or made available to someone who can do it in less time hence using less fuel. You may of course steal it but you risk retaliation from those from whom you want to steal and in the case of an organized society by the authority given its governing body by its citizens to prevent and punish theft.

Theft

There are many forms of theft; overt and covert. Since overt theft is easily recognized as are felonies such as embezzlement and fraud the only ones that need be described are those either encouraged or sanctioned by the very government we have instituted to prevent and punish it. These are certain forms of extortion which manifest themselves in the form of usury and result from obtaining a monopoly position either through subterfuge or direct government action.

In simple terms usury is making money on money or as defined by Webster as charging an excessive amount of interest on a loan. If there is money available in a bank not being currently invested in income producing assets the only cost to the bank is the labor it takes to assemble the money and service it through the receipt of payments. If there is a balloon payment only at the end of the loan period even this is reduced. The servicing of a $10,000 loan and one of $1,000,000 is exactly the same but if interest is applied equally to each only the amount of the theft is greater.

Monopolies, in and of themselves are good because they are hard to achieve when competition is encouraged they result in the lowest cost to the consumer in the markets they serve. Issuance by government of protections for intellectual property in the form of patents and copyrights for certain periods of time enable their recipients to charge whatever the traffic will bear for their output until these rights expire. It also encourages potential competitors to introduce nearly equal substitutes (knockoffs) resulting in legal battles to defend one's monopoly protection. The entire matter can be avoided, including the legal battles by taxing away any excess income earned between the lowest selling price and that currently being charged. In addition, the company executive who sanctioned the increase would be punished for theft.

Much more common are individual monopoly practices that are not even recognized as such. Their manifestation is in the exorbitant amount paid to individual performers in the entertainment industry that includes sports figures. It is the consequence of giving unions and their members bargaining power without any recourse to the employer other than to do without. It is foolhardy to say the U. S. Constitution specifically prohibits the States from impairing the obligations of contracts and does not give such power to the Congress when in fact they have and when the Roosevelt Administration passed such legislation and when it was challenged the Supreme Court made up of Roosevelt appointees sanctioned it. It is difficult to understand how we can have a country governed by the rule of law when the law makers can make laws for which they were never given power and to make laws specifically prohibited.

Competition

If everyone is given currency equivalent to the kcal being produced the amount of that currency is limited only by the amount of land allocated to its production and is therefore finite. It becomes the amount available to those who provide the services necessary or desirable by the people who cannot or choose not to participate in the workforce. It has been shown that the maximum amount is equal to the distribution beyond which the individual will either perform the task himself or obtain the service from someone else because even if he has a monopoly he cannot charge more than the last price charged when he was in competition. This is even made more unlikely by the advent of machinery to replace human labor. The other incentive to produce salable work is that it is the only way by which one can improve their lifestyle.

The first question one must ask is what is the effect on this economy by the engagement of people who operate under the current economy where one has to work in order to survive? In one case the individual is given his kcal and in the other case he must earn it. In the first case all the kcal is spent to obtain the lifestyle associated with having so many kcal and in the latter case he must work to obtain the same lifestyle as the first. This disincentive is overcome when one is given charity either by individuals or government. Why work when you can survive without it? It is the reason the United States and other countries with elaborate welfare systems are magnets for those seeking paid employment or even slave labor in order to survive. It is absurd that the government and private charities provide food or the wherewithal to buy it and then take it away when one does seek and find employment when not everyone can be employed. Compounding this condition is the encouragement for the county's youth to become educated to perform jobs that unless in government or subsidized by it are rapidly being eliminated where they can be in the private sector. It is not an economic system that is destined for survival.

There is only so much exchange available and that in order to obtain it one must perform work the output of which someone needs or wants. That the lowest wage or salary is guaranteed by the system described can be proven by the fact that given the distribution of the equivalent for survival some people will work for nothing. Most people must work because no one can survive on their own and improvement in lifestyle is possible only if one works. If, as posited, a man spent all his time doing for himself and one who could not the most he could earn is what he is given in the distribution and what he is paid is from the distribution of the one for whom he is providing all the services. If he attempted to demand more he would be immediately challenged by someone who would accept less or nothing.

The Economy

Webster defines the economy as the "management of income and expenditures". When I was taught economics the value of a company was determined by its ability to produce a product or service such that its projected income would return sufficient revenue to return its capital investment and provide the maximum return to the owners to justify or encourage their investment. It also means it could all be lost if one guessed wrong, a risk one takes to improve one's life style and the society as a whole. As the earth provides sufficient kcal for all those currently alive the consequences of taking risks should not be starvation. Except for charity both private and government that is exactly the downside risk in an economy where one must spend their time in compensated work or investment. It becomes inevitable when the kcal required exceeds the kcal being produced and there will be no more places one can go where this is not the case. The economic models that have been adopted by every government to date have built in this inevitability by unequally distributing nature's wealth. This has been accomplished by allowing theft by some or the many when it is constituted solely to prevent and punish it.

There are no more deserted islands that provide the ability of the number of humans currently inhabiting the planet to survive without the effort of others but it can be earned by exchanging your labor or the fruits of it for the fuel necessary for survival. Even the farmer cannot escape the consequences of increases in population because he must produce and sell his surplus output in order to buy the tools and equipment in order to produce it. He can only sell it, if there is a market for his output and his price is equal to or less than his competitor. For others this presupposes that your labor is available and either desired or needed and you have not already taken on an obligation to provide for others such as a spouse or children or elderly parents. For such a system to work there first must be sufficient fuel available for everyone to survive. Secondly, there must be a proxy for the fuel necessary to sustain life as it is consumed or it will rot if not consumed. The proxy must be equivalent to the energy content of food and like food itself reproducible. If, as James Mason has said, "all men are created equal under the law" and if there is to be no stealing, each member of a law abiding society, each member of that society shall share equally, up front, the fruits of nature, with man's help has provided. Thomas Jefferson incorporated part of this in the Declaration of Independence but omitted the part that restricted it to the law.

This process is called natural evolution and can function efficiently only on condition that nature's assets are shared equally and the only thing that belongs to the individual is the result of the fruits of one's labor. Because we all require fuel (food) to sustain life and produce the energy for work and not everyone is able to work, sharing, imposed by our dependency on each other, is the only means to insure survival.

Summary

The foregoing discussion was intended to prove that the only real inherent difference between individuals is the amount of fuel they need for survival and that difference is insignificant and related solely to the physical capacity of the body as determined by hereditary characteristics passed on by ones parents. Marked differences in physical or mental output are the consequences of training and practice and the maximum difference between the norm and that of the experienced

THE REAL ECONOMY

(trained and practiced) is twice that of the norm. Survival is dependent on the availability of sufficient fuel. The ability to improve one's style of life is totally dependent on the availability of opportunities to provide products or services others need or want in fair competition with those offering to supply them. Fair competition exists in an environment where theft in any form is prohibited, unrewarded and punished. Society itself defines theft and those selected to exercise the police power to prevent, apprehend and punish theft may not exempt themselves or others from any form of it and be punished themselves for doing so.

2
PROXIES AS EXCHANGE

The Metal Proxy

History records the adoption of gold and silver as proxies or currencies that could be used in trade and to manage an economy. These were metals that were more decorative than utilitarian, as substitutes such as iron or bronze were much more suitable for tools and weapons. They were also available in all societies that had advanced to where the volume and character of trade were such that a proxy for food, the primary trade commodity was needed. It also meant that whoever owned the land on which the gold or silver was found and mined it became rich. How rich depended on the market value of the gold or silver.

It has been mentioned that any proxy for food must have the characteristics of reproducibility and be consumable. What is not consumed can be saved and added to that produced in the next cycle. The reason these characteristics are necessary is that what one is buying with the proxy is not the food itself but its fuel value less the fuel consumed by the labor that produced it. Nature has provided it free to the one who cultivates and harvests it. Neither gold nor silver have any of these characteristics and even if its value has been imputed it will have to be changed when the cost of its production exceeds that of its market value. Paper currency can serve as a proxy for gold or silver only if the gold for which it is issued is taken out of circulation.

All countries of the ancient world had gold and in its pure form the only way to tell which country the gold came from is to examine the trace elements that could not be completely eliminated due to refining, a technique not developed until centuries later. When gold came into use as a proxy arbitragers were quick to take advantage of the fact the cost to actually produce an ounce of gold in one place was different from that of another, a factor called arbitrage. Paper money, as a more convenient substitute for gold did not eliminate this arbitrage opportunity. In simple terms it was making money on money without adding any value through human effort.

Arbitrage, like charging interest on loans by charging a percentage instead of the actual cost of the effort to accumulate the desired amount and administer its repayment is stealing. The Christian Bible tells the story of Jesus running the money changers out of the temple for this very reason. When this arbitrage occurred it should have become obvious that gold was a poor proxy for something that had the characteristics necessary for external trade. Mine owners, the holders of gold and the moneychangers could not let this windfall disappear. They assured the practice would not be stopped and was not prosecuted by the governments they supported.

Take for example at mine A the cost to the mine owner to mine and smelt an ounce of gold was one quarter of an ounce for slave labor, equipment and profit. At mine B that same ounce of gold cost its owner one half of an ounce. The gold was the same but the cost to produce it was twice as much. If used as currency to buy anything its equivalent was whatever one was willing to trade for it, say one ounce would buy a bushel of apples. Therefore, one ounce of gold would equal 1 bushel of apples. So long as the cost to mine it did not exceed its cost the only difference was the excess the owner of A had over B which, because his gold cost only half as much. This difference is arbitrage. The economy of the country in which A and B reside and trade is then measured by the cost in manhours of the gold being produced. A bushel of apples will always be a bushel of apples but the value of an ounce of gold will not because nature does not reproduce what is mined and smelted. As supplies dwindle the cost to mine and smelt it increases due to the amount of other minerals contained in the various ores until the cost to mine it exceeds its market value and the arbitrage disappears putting the highest cost producer out of business unless its price rises with its scarcity.

An increase in the population also increases the volume of exchange. Learning to cultivate the land reduced the need for migration and tribes were no longer required to be nomadic in search of food. The common ownership and equal distribution of the means of production was evolving into a system of ownership and the control and the management of the life economy was vested in those who owned the land producing the food and the style economy everything else. The style economy has now become predominant because whatever exchange is used to measure the economy, unlike food, is spent but not consumed by the individual so it accumulates and depreciates over time until it is totally consumed or discarded. Agricultural producers were losing control of the economy to the mercantilists. Because of the arbitrage factor those who have the exchange accumulate the most of it. All governments to date have perpetuated this system of legalized theft and their duration is dependent only on how long they can control the people they subjugate. When the government fails instead of replacing it with an economic system that evenly distributes nature's riches the participants merely change places. The distribution of wealth has taken many forms; communism, socialism, fascism, democracy and republicanism. Only the latter, that distributes wealth evenly, has never been tried. The framers of the United States Constitution made an attempt to create a Republic but adopted the British model economic system that allowed usury by the banks thereby dooming it to ultimate failure.

It has been shown that gold serves as a poor proxy for equating exchanges so it was wishful thinking that paper currency based on gold could magically be imbued with the characteristics that gold lacked. On the contrary, it magnified it. As the cost to mine and smelt gold in the ancient world kept rising, people began migrating again because in order to survive they had to work but didn't earn enough to satisfy their needs through sharing so they had to find new sources of earnings. Those who had the excess exchange and were not forced or encouraged by government or their conscience to give up their surplus they spent it on themselves first to insure their survival and then to enhance their style of life. Fortunately for some migrants they found areas sparsely populated and peoples who still lived as migrants and were either willing to share the surplus nature provided them. If they did have unmined gold, did nothing with it because it had no useful purpose and you could not eat it. It is what the Europeans found when they ventured to North America. What they found in Central America and parts of South America was gold accumulated by other societies that did mine it. They stole both and the arbitragers flourished and countries like England, France, Portugal and Spain flourished with the new found gold.

The emigrants usually moved into areas that not only had surplus land but had not advanced past the barter stage of commerce. They did not yet need a proxy and most did not even know they had gold unless it was in nearly pure nugget form. Some of the emigrants were actually prospectors looking for it and snatched up the most promising sites. True to form, the arbitragers bought up the properties of the small holders eager for instant riches or merely stole them. Much of it was in a form requiring less cost to produce than that from places they left. As a consequence they automatically replaced our previous miner A in respect to the amount of arbitrage they could command. North America became the last frontier for gold arbitragers. The economy fails, not when the gold runs out, but when the economy consumes all that is produced and there is none remaining to reproduce a like amount.

The Paper Proxy

The industrial revolution, the rapid increase in population and the shift of the western world from an agrarian to an industrial basis sounded the death knell of gold and gold backed paper as a medium of commercial exchange. The discovery of huge deposits of gold and silver in the western United States was shifting the arbitrage in gold from England to the United States in the second half of the nineteenth century. By the start of the twentieth the dollar had already arrested leadership from the £ Sterling Its supremacy was punctuated by World War I that saw the beginning of the end of the British Empire and British leadership in the industrial economy that was rapidly advancing throughout Europe and in particular the United States.

Table 1 illustrates the change in gold prices over most of the history of the United States. The establishment of a formal $ price for gold coincides closely with the shift in the English population's shift from a life economy to a style economy resulting from the Industrial Revolution. Heretofore the colonies operated on the basis of a barter or life economy. It continued as such until well after the Revolution except it now had an official measure. Gold was finally discovered in North Carolina in 1793 but in very limited quantities until vast reserves were discovered in California in 1848 and later in Alaska. America then became the arbitrager of gold as well as silver.

Table 1: HISTORICAL GOLD PRICES- 1833 to Present

1833-49*	$18.93	1940	$33.85
1850	$18.93	1950	$34.72
1860	$18.93	1960	$35.27
1870	$18.93	1970	$36.02
1880	$18.94	1980	$615.00
1890	$18.94	1990**	$383.51
1900	$18.96	2000	$279.11
1910	$18.92	2010	$1224.53
1920	$20.68		
1930	$20.65		

* Prices from 1883-1994, World Gold Council
**Prices from 1995, Kitco.com

THE REAL ECONOMY

The increase in 1834 came as a result of the Industrial Revolution that started in England and began the massive shift in the British economy to a style economy. The upshot in the change was that the benefits of the style economy were less than anticipated because the Revolution ended the tax collection on the colonists coupled with the loss of a large market as American manufacturers began replacing what was heretofore imported. By 1834 the imputed value of gold was set by the Americans who were driving the life and style economy in lock step right up to World War I. It came to a screeching halt in 1933, not as a result of the stock market crash of 1929 but because of an abrupt downturn in the life economy when production of wheat dropped by over 30% in less than two years.

The collapse of agriculture production should have been a wakeup call that that there was something structurally wrong with an economic system that enables a select few to obtain massive wealth, a large portion of the population to have their cake and eat it too and the remainder to subsist on charity. Instead of at a minimum leaving a sick beast to get well on its own the government undertook policies that continue to make matters worse and then enacted laws found constitutional when challenged, that insure they will.

The backing for the dollar is now claimed to be "the full faith and credit of the United States". I posit that it is the kcal because the United States is one of the last countries that produce the fuel necessary for life in quantities excess to the needs of its population and currently feeds a goodly portion of the world's population.

Two events in the first half of the nineteenth century should have exposed first gold and then the gold backed U. S. dollar as a poor proxy for what actually fuels the life and style economies and that is the kcal value of its agriculture. The first was the 1929 stock market crash. The United States was the new frontier of opportunity. Europe had become saturated and its arbitrage dwindling because of the constant discovery of new and less expensively produced gold in the Dakotas, California, and Alaska and silver in Nevada. Speculators were anxious to cash in on the markets brought on by the rapid demand created by the millions of immigrants pouring into the country. The U. S. Population grew by over 62% between the years 1900 and 1930. The arbitragers were all too happy to loan their dollars to the speculators because the collateral, they got was not real estate or fixed assets they had to sell but dollars in the form of liquid assets (securities). Market rules allowed short sales meaning money could be made when the price of a stock went up or down meaning the lenders bore no risk. It was the speculators who went bankrupt when the real value of their assets was eclipsed by the speculative value that could not be supported by their ability to repay their debts, very similar to the situation that would overtake the farmers in less than a decade. The value of the land would soon recover; the value of the stocks would not.

The second event was the "Great Depression". Its cause was poor agricultural practices coupled with weather conditions that resulted in several years of severely reduced crop production in the Midwestern states. Wheat production, for example, dropped 20% between 1931 and 1932 and another 27% the following year. It continued to drop but began turning around in 1935. When you don't harvest it you do not have to ship it, you don't have to process it and you can't make bread, cakes and other wheat based commodities from nothing. As a consequence farmers lost their land because they had no income to pay their debts and the trickledown effect of the loss of raw material caused massive job losses in both direct and indirect businesses dependent on the grain industry.

There was enough grain to feed the population because a large portion of the crop was being exported primarily to feed Europe but those unemployed needed the money to buy it. When they made a run for their savings the banks did not have it all because much of it had been loaned. Not only did many banks fail but the mortgages they held on farmland lost their value when the farmers could not pay them. Whether the American people could have weathered the depression with private charity will probably never be known but a goodly number did because they migrated to where there were still opportunities, particularly in California.

The Irish Potato Famine of 1845-49 is a classic case where the economy of the working classes was based on the kcal of the potato. Grains were sufficient to weather the storm but those who owned it continued to export it and turn it into alcohol resulting in a significant migration of the population, primarily to the United States. A similar fate would await the United States were it not for public welfare payments and private charity but we would have nowhere to go and would have to resort to theft. It is a sad state of affairs when criminals fare better than law-abiding citizens who live in poverty.

Gold or silver does not qualify but can function in the capacity of a proxy so long as its imputed value is higher than the value it took to produce it. It has been shown that even within an individual country's economy; the actual value of gold can be different enabling arbitrage. When trade or commerce extends to other countries with an even lower cost of production arbitrage could be exploited between countries. Paper currency does not eliminate arbitrage if it is tied to anything but the kcal. That will occur only under the conditions already described. Paper money however requires less storage space and its value can be easily changed just by putting on bigger numbers. Germany after World War I and countries such as Brazil and Argentina illustrate this problem.

Every country must trade in order to enjoy a lifestyle above mere survival. Germany incurred a huge debt as a consequence of losing World War I and agreed to onerous reparations payments. At first it refused to pay them and the French tried to force payment by occupying parts of Germany resulting in a new agreement stretching the payments and

PROXIES AS EXCHANGE

arranging international loans which only added to the amount. Unable to tax the people to pay the debt and still stay in power the government resorted to printing money ostensibly revaluing the gold it had and was paying out. Mathematically this is not a straight line process but an exponential one and the shorter the time it takes to reach the tipping point where the economy collapses and the government changes and restructures the economy. In Germany's case they revalued the German Mark and stopped paying the debt. The U. S. and other countries that provide government welfare or entitlements cannot solve the problem in this manner because the debt keeps increasing with the number of individuals requiring it.

Brazil on the other hand lives from hand to mouth and like other countries whose agriculture still produces sufficient food the government, like that of 1920s Germany refused to tax itself out of power and started printing currency causing rampant inflation followed by toppling of the government and revaluation . This process has been repeated several times. They still produce a huge kcal surplus in the form of sugar but one cannot live on sugar alone and most of its surplus is now converted to ethanol which enables them to reduce somewhat their purchases of foreign oil and brings a higher margin than that of sugar. In the United States we use subsidized corn to produce subsidized ethanol to replace the oil we do not produce the price of which is determined by the members of OPEC but particularly Saudi Arabia.

Israel is teetering on the brink of collapse. It produces just enough to satisfy the needs of its people and yet is still increasing its population. It has resorted to selling what it produces in the form of higher labor content foods to Europe in order to obtain the exchange to buy wheat which has much higher kcal and lesser labor content than the food they sell. The shortfall for the Jewish population is made up of charity primarily from the United States and for the Muslim population by countries like Saudi Arabia and Kuwait who would prefer they stay where they are rather than immigrate to their countries and become permanent societal burdens. In addition the United Nations subsidizes those living in the refugee camps in the Gaza Strip.

The United States has taken a different approach preferring to accept the immigrants rather than feed them in their own country. The reason is the experience that aid, in whatever form is accepted by the country receiving it is on condition that they control its distribution which results in the bulk of it being given to the ones who keep them in power. This means those needing it most are the ones who rarely get it and if they do pay dearly for it in one form or another. When a person must work to live and there is no work or prospect of any the need for charity can never be slaked and becomes a permanent factor unless one immigrates to where the food or the charity to provide it is direct. The United States has not learned this lesson and as a consequence has adopted the most expensive way to solve a problem that will never go away and will get worse under the present economic system.

It is well to mention countries like Kuwait, Saudi Arabia, Qatar and the United Arab Emirates. None of the them produce anywhere near the food necessary to feed their populations, let alone the millions of foreigners they have brought in to do most of the work. Because they had no more gold or silver to arbitrage the industrial age bailed them out of virtual oblivion to the extent they now possess the new proxy for gold and silver for the arbitragers and that is crude oil. They are employing arbitrage to the hilt because they have formed a monopoly and can manipulate the price to keep out other producers. Their governments are stable because they share enough of the wealth they are earning to provide every one of their citizens a handsome life style whether they work or not. Because they are in a world economy measured by the dollar they cannot allow the United States who manufactures the dollars to go bankrupt. The U. S. dollar is now the world's reserve currency, the dollar having replaced gold as the means of exchange.

PROXIES AS EXCHANGE

In addition to illustrating why gold or any other non-reproducible element cannot serve as a proxy for the fuel value of food, it illustrates the significant changes in our economic history. It was Sir Isaac Newton as master of the United Kingdom mint that set the £ price for gold in 1717. It remained that for two hundred years until 1914. The $ price of gold started at $19.75 in 1792 when the $ replaced the £ as the official medium of exchange. It was raised to $20.67 in 1834 and to $35 in 1934. It was raised again in 1972 to $38 and again in 1973 to $42.22. A two tier system was created in 1968 and allowed to float freely determined by the market in 1973 when President Nixon officially took the United States off the gold standard.

The interesting and significant facet of this price development is its coincidence with the shift of the population from an economy based on reproducible assets to one based on non-reproducible assets that can be accumulated like the proxy that serves to fuel them. A proxy can accumulate and retain its value in the life economy only so long as its fuel value in the life economy is less than that in the style economy. In other words it can serve as a proxy only so long as the actual cost to produce it is less than or equal to its actual value.

3
TWO ECONOMIES ONE MEANS OF EXCHANGE

We live in a world with two economies. These are the life economy and the style economy. The life economy is that in which man lives in the state of Adam. That is, everything he needs and wants is provided by him and nature. The life economy is that which makes the style economy possible. That is, man can no longer live in the state of Adam but must rely on others to augment nature, process its fruits and distribute them. The only measure of exchange that ties the two economies together is the kcal or kilogram-calorie abundant in all foods. It is the only measure of constant value and reproducible to the extent necessary to sustain life.

The problem is that man requires a continuous input of calories that can only be satisfied by his fellow man. In short, man cannot subsist on his own unless he performs all of the necessary effort to cultivate, harvest, process and distribute the kcal provided by nature. He needs a system that utilizes the efforts of his fellow citizens to provide the kcal and the wherewithal and style by which they are provided. That system is free market capitalism.

The argument for free market capitalism is based on several assumptions. First, that all of earth's natural resources are finite and its renewable assets are intimately interconnected with its non-renewable assets. Second, that all life on earth will cease when any one the factors necessary to life; air, water, food, and light, are insufficient. Thirdly, the rate at which all human life will disappear is dependent on man's consumption of things he or nature cannot reproduce.

Thanks to the bounty supplied by nature man has been able to multiply while at the same time enhance nature and develop tools to relieve the physical burdens of existence and hence to maintain the number of kcal necessary for survival. Growing numbers have led to the division of labor increasing the volume of exchanges. Barter sufficed when the numbers were small and as they grew common commodities were used. Further growth in numbers caused the link between man and the means of his survival to be inextricably broken and if man was to obtain those things essential to life he then had to barter his time in order to survive.

The problem with non-renewable materials as a means of exchange is they are not linked to life itself and lack the qualities of being reproducible and of constant value. Paper money is the only medium that serves that purpose in the volume required and only if the value printed on it is based on the kcal. It will not have that value if the society using it is incapable of producing it and in order to survive must steal, individually or collectively through war. It is the energy present in all foods which sustain life and provide the energy necessary to produce work. It is not affected by political subdivisions and because it is crucial to life suffices to measure both production and consumption.

Only nature can provide kcal and it does so through the production of living things. Man consumes some of those kcal and those that are surplus to his needs are consumed by other living things or goes to waste. The kcal used to convert non-reproducible commodities for trade may accumulate and be resold sometimes for hundreds of years but are subject to rules preventing theft that will be discussed in the next chapter.

Man's numbers and distribution throughout the planet require that to be self-sufficient in the current economic system man must obtain those kcal by employing his human capital, first to insure survival and then to obtain material things produced by himself or others. The kcal is the measure that can be used first to value that which man needs for survival and to value the output of his human capital.

The expected life span of man is approximately 70 years or 25,550 days. If he consumes 2500 kcal per day he will have to acquire at least as much as he consumes. The first 15 years of life will be consumed in preparing for employment and the last 15 retired or unemployable. Survival requires man obtain food, water, clothing and shelter. If he obtains these through the efforts of others he will have to acquire enough to buy the time of others providing these services which means he will have to support at least one other man in order to obtain his 2500 kcal.

Unlike other animals, man spends a decreasing amount of his human capital obtaining his kcal requirements leaving either more time for leisure or producing things other people need or want to enhance their lifestyle. Conversely, he can use his human capital to procure the things he wants from others. What we have then are two economies, one for survival alone and another for style or manner of living both measured in kcal.

Just as all foods have different kcal content, human capital has different values; generic or acquired. It is relatively easy to measure the kcal content of various foods. Even if they vary over time it is miniscule and can be adjusted accordingly. It was easier to measure the kcal value of human capital only to know that it is not the same for every individual but its limit is about 2500 kcal/day. In addition, opportunity is also a factor in the ability to employ it. If a society is to be benevolent and compassionate it will also provide for those who are unable to produce and can only consume. With the exception of the latter, the remainder of the society must participate in the style economy in order to participate in the life economy. If we call this the free market capitalist model we need define its parameters and the rules for its implementation. The problems started when those who devised a system to administer it devised one that contained a fatal flaw that like a hidden virus took time to be exposed and when exposed was allowed to metastasize and when cures were tried they only made matters worse.

The Fatal Flaw

Life is a zero sum game; you start with nothing and end with nothing. Along the way you obtain and spend nature's fuel to sustain life. You cannot consume more than is produced without consequence and that consequence is dilution of means of exchange. Nor, can you have your cake and eat it too. If you create a proxy for the fuel of life (kcal) and use it as a means of exchange the proxy accumulates so there must be rules for its use such that once it is spent by the individual that possesses it cannot be spent again.

If you are given 1,000,000 kcals each year you can spend it all or save some of it for future use. Let us say you save 100,000 and it resides in your bank account. The bank loans this money on a promise of the borrower to pay it back over a certain period. This puts the 100,000 in circulation and is spent by the borrower. If the depositor wants to spend his savings before the loan is repaid he will not be able to get it back because it is no longer in his account. This is what occurred during the Great Depression. In other words, you cannot have your cake and eat it too. It occurs in a micro manner each time there is a default on a loan and so long as the bank continues to make usurious profits can absorb a modest amount of losses because all they do is reduce the amount of profit.

After the Great Depression the banks created the Federal Deposit Insurance Corporation to insure the banks could weather another storm by guaranteeing bank deposits. In addition, the government established Fannie Mae and Freddie Mac, two lending agencies that bought mortgages issued by the banks and securitized them enabling banks to further their lending efforts, again putting exchange into circulation that would not be actually be generated until future years further diluting the value of that in circulation.

Borrowing, or spending money you do not have results in inflation of the means of exchange. Even if you pay it back in full the damage is irreversible. It has gone unnoticed because unlike Germany after World War I where its exchange was being revalued on almost a daily basis because the government was merely printing money; it has been incrementally slow, averaging only about 3% per year. Nevertheless, it is accelerating because Americans are no longer saving and more and more are living on government welfare and others on payday loans which exacerbate the problem.

When the framers of our Constitution went about correcting the shortfalls of the Articles of Confederation the first thing they did was give the Congress the power to tax to pay for the operations of the federal government. This was done so that the country would never again turn in to a debtor nation. There was no need for a balanced budget under which the States had to operate because the federal government could recover expenditures as they were incurred. In emergencies, such as occurred during the Revolution, the Congress was given a second power that of borrowing to meet unexpected needs. That borrowing was intended to come from the people's unspent savings and to be repaid without interest, much the same as a bank loan should have been without the fee and without usury. After all they were borrowing from themselves and need pay no fee for the service. Because we had adopted the British system wherein the banks were an intermediary they quickly jumped at the opportunity to buy the nation's debt that could not be recovered with taxes, charged a fee and made a usurious profit exposing the fatal flaw that the ultimate addition of currency to the system dilutes its value and cannot be reversed. The banks had ultimate control over the economy.

TWO ECONOMIES ONE MEANS OF EXCHANGE

The formula for survival can be written:

$$\frac{P}{912{,}500[(x-y)(1+i)^t]} - 1 = 0 \qquad \text{Equation (1)}$$

Production (P) is the total amount of kcal produced; (x) is the number of individuals in the style economy and (y) the number of individuals in the life economy. The constant 912.500 is the number of kcal the (y) population must produce in order to support him and at least one (x). The term (i) is the targeted growth rate as measured by the medium of exchange. Time (t) is sidereal time of one year signifying the annual growth cycle of nature's reproducible food crops. Substitution of actual numbers in this equation will demonstrate that (x) must always be greater than 0 if the human race is to survive through reproduction. Solving for the production requirements yields the equation:

$$P = 912{,}500[(x-y)(1+i)^t] \qquad \text{Equation (2)}$$

It should be obvious that if (i) is greater than 0, P must increase correspondingly. Stability is reached after (i) reaches 0 and declines when (i) is negative. This is the economic system we were taught where the various phases of a corporation were growth, maturity and ultimate decline. In this case P represents total sales, (x) the sales price, (y) the cost of sales and (1+i) the profit on sales. Growth meant (i) was positive, maturity when (i) was 0 and when (x) finally equaled (y) a further slide was irreversible.

If the human race is to survive it must do so in groups of at least six. The reason is that the female is only capable of reproduction for a period of about 28 years. We know a female can conceive at about the age of 12 but it is doubtful she or the child would survive because her body is not yet fully grown and the physical atributes probably incapable of surviving childbirth. Under normal circumstances then this period would be reduced to about 24. What this means is that for about one-third of her life a female must consume enough food for two if she is to have a child each birthing cycle and conceives a child who will be a dependent for at least a third of their life. As man has no enemy other than other humans a family of six need have only three producers so long as there is sufficient kcal for six and two of the females capable of reproduction produce at least one child each of a different sex. This exact same pattern exists throughout the animal kingdom. As no rules prevail for the rest of the animal kingdom the multiplication is self-controlling when the numbers exceed the capacity of the food system. Humans, who are capable of self-governance, have refused to establish rules to limit reproduction and on the contrary establish policies that encourage it. Like other animals when there is not enough food to go around they tend to migrate where it is in surplus or steal it from those who have it. In the end they kill each other for it.

The variable (x) is itself a multiple variable. There are those who do not work and are entirely dependent on charity for their survival I will call (d). There are those that previously worked and are entirely dependent on government charity (tax revenue) for their survival I will call (g). Then there are those who work and who receive government subsidies in one form or another, again from tax revenue I will call (s). Then there are those who work in what is the so-called private sector I will call (p). The equation then revised to where it becomes:

$$P = 912{,}500\{[(d+g+s+p)-y](1+i)^t\} \qquad \text{Equation (3)}$$

The basic measure of P, the kcal, is variable but its amount is limited only by the amount being consumed because it is reproducible. It is only reproducible if a surplus is produced in order to reproduce a like amount the following growing cycle. In the case of wheat, for example, the excess is 6% of the total crop that when planted will produce the same amount the following year, all other things such as water and soil nutrients being replaced.

These are all variables and unfortunately the economy not the government can control most of the numbers. The number of children born

TWO ECONOMIES ONE MEANS OF EXCHANGE

to legal residents who make up (d) is decreasing as attested by the census because the population is aging, more so in some states as opposed to others. The number of people represented by (g) is increasing and includes all Social Security recipients including retirees who paid into the system and whose money has been spent and whose benefits now come from current dollars acquired by the government through taxes. There is another component of (d) and that is the so called "homeless" who have fallen through the crack and do not qualify for government aid and rely on private charity for their survival. This number is growing and the government has no way to really find them or devised a system to help. The number represented by (s) is growing in leaps and bounds as more government jobs are retained and more jobs created that were once in the private sector. I cite the establishment of the Homeland Security Department as only one but the government entirely supports the Military Industrial Complex of firms that are the most pernicious in that we even loan money to countries in order for them to buy the products they produce. It also includes the entire legal and accounting profession that are engaged in either conforming to government regulation or finding a way to thwart them. It also includes the entire insurance industry which under the economic system later described would be unnecessary. The number in (p) is made up of the many small individually owned businesses that although they must conform to the same regulations as their larger brethren are exempt from the federal but not necessarily the state's minimum wage laws. It is safe to say the gap between the numbers of people who depend on tax revenue as opposed to those paying it is widening in terms of current dollars as evidenced by the amount of borrowing by the government as opposed to taxation that is constitutionally required.

When you put a proxy as a substitute for the basic value of P the equation becomes simply:

$$P - (gold\ or\ £\ or\ \$) = 0$$

None of these proxies, in particular gold, have the property of reproduction with their real value remaining constant. Gold is limited in supply and as that supply is consumed each ounce becomes costlier in terms of manhours to produce. As populations expanded and newer sources were found arbitrage became possible. When the last arbitrager gave up using it as a medium of exchange because there was an insufficient supply to sustain the growing volume of commerce the substitute became the £ and then the $ whose volume is limited only by the numbers printed on it but whose value in the next cycle will be zero when the amount needed to be issued equals P less the amount necessary to reproduce itself.

The fatal flaw was hard to detect because it was kept hiding behind disguises. The first disguise was gold and silver. Then it was the £. Now it is the $. It would still have been elusive was it not for the fact that it has now been exposed. The problem now that it has been exposed is to convince an always suspecting public that it really is why governments fall. The following table will do just that because it is proof of the validity of Equation (1).

The data shown comes from a much larger data set that includes all of the interim years which have been removed so as to allow the data to be presented on a single page. The cumulative effect of using a proxy that retains its value with its consumption by individuals is disguised when its imputed value is greater than its real value. What is illustrated by the table is why they do not work, not how. The difference in total inflation as given here and that in the commonly used "Inflation Clock" available on the internet is that it does not included collateralized borrowing for housing.

The American colonies monetary system was the same as that of Great Britain that was based on the British Sterling Pound (£). The £ was tied to gold because by the 1600s the British controlled the arbitrage in gold and could set its price in the world market. The establishment

TWO ECONOMIES ONE MEANS OF EXCHANGE

Year	GDP Millions	Federal Debt Millions	Trade Deficit Millions	Personal Debt Millions	Annual Inflation	Cum. Inflation
1915	39,048	-1,095	0	0	0.00	-0.06
1920	89,246	0	0	0	0.00	-0.06
1925	91,449	0	0	0	0.00	-0.06
1930	92,200	0	0	0	0.00	-0.06
1935	74,300	-2,803	0	0	-0.04	-0.25
1940	102,900	-2,920	0	0	-0.03	-0.38
1945	228,200	-15,936	0	-6,800	-0.10	-1.18
1950	300,200	-3,119	0	-23,947	-0.09	-1.49
1955	426,200	-2,993	0	-42,949	-0.11	-1.96
1960	543,300	0	3,508	-61,248	-0.11	-2.52
1965	743,700	-1,411	4,664	-97,489	-0.13	-3.13
1970	1,075,900	-2,842	2,254	-133,660	-0.12	-3.80
1975	1,688,900	-53,242	12,404	-206,996	-0.15	-4.53
1980	2,862,500	-73,830	-19,407	-358,044	-0.16	-5.34
1985	4,346,700	-212,308	-121,880	-610,574	-0.22	-6.27
1990	5,979,600	-221,227	-80,864	-824,391	-0.19	-7.27
1995	7,664,100	-163,952	-96,384	-1,168,160	-0.19	-8.17
2000	10,284,800	0	-372,517	-1,741,267	-0.21	-9.31
2005	13,093,700	-318,346	-714,245	-2,320,564	-0.26	-10.32
2010	14,964,400	-1,294,373	-494,658	-2,646,898	-0.30	-11.67
2015	18,007,328	-582,505	-531,503	-3,546,855	-0.26	-13.01

Table 2- U. S. Dollar Inflation-GDP and deficit data from U.S. Office of Management and Budget.

of a U. S. Government did not change that condition until gold and silver were discovered in vast quantities in the western United States. Until the Revolutionary war the colonies had little need for any more gold than they obtained from the sale of surplus agricultural products mostly England. The vast majority of the population lived on the land, produced what they needed from the land and bartered with their neighbors for what excess they could produce. As such they had little need of a formal style market and hence little need for gold or the currency used as exchange. The fact that over 90% of the population lived on the land should attest to this assumption.

If this assumption is correct and it is proven by the consequences of its diminution over time, then an assumption for the determination of the minimum wage for those working in the style economy should be equally correct. If this is true, it does not matter at which point in time is selected to illustrate the consequences of the uses of a medium of exchange that accumulates over time. Also, more data is available from reliable sources the closer one gets to current history. For the purposes of this study the year 1914 was selected as the base year in order to establish a nominal cost of the kcal. In that year, the price of a bushel of wheat, one of the most efficient producers of kcal of all grains produced in sufficient quantity to supply the necessary kcal to feed the population was $1.00. Production was 900 million bushels of wheat on 55 million acres at about 15 bushels per acre of which 335 million bushels were exported. The nominal cost of 912,500 kcal, the annual need of the average person, works out to a cost of $13.66 per year. This cannot be the minimum wage because a person's diet is made up of other grains, fruits and vegetables and liquids all of which are of higher cost and lower kcal per unit of weight. In addition man requires other necessities, that of clothing and shelter.

In 2015 the yield had risen to over 2 billion bushels on the same acreage with the average yield per acre rising to 44 bu./acre. The price however had risen to $5.00 per bushel making our 912,500 kcal cost a nominal $68.00 per year. The yield efficiency had been entirely due to improvements in the genetic makeup of the seeds, fertilization to replace the soils nutrients and provide more than were being taken up by the individual seeds, the application of pesticides and irrigation. Most of these become constants that are a onetime cost of production as does the use of machinery in planting and harvesting. Not so the increase in the cost of labor. It is subject to the natural inflation of the currency as well as government legislation. What was happening was the efficiency induced by human labor was being partially offset by the need for higher production due to the increasing number of mouths to feed and the shift of the larger portion of the population into the style

TWO ECONOMIES ONE MEANS OF EXCHANGE

economy and the money thereby made available for a shift that always saw these most efficient kcal producers actually requiring subsidies to produce them or farmers would shift to more profitable kcal producers as opposed to the most efficient.

The term minimum wage is oxymoronic. First there must be a demand for jobs that pay it and it must be increased to conform to inflation of the currency due to borrowing or outright printing resulting from a failure to tax. The minimum need in terms of the kcal is 912,500 and is constant whatever the value of the currency. If you wanted to create more jobs it would make sense to cap the maximum wage that in kcal terms would be 1,825,000 kcal. In a perfect world of groups of 6, half of them need produce a surplus of 2,737,500 kcal in order for all 6 to obtain their needs. The critical assumption here is that sufficient surplus can be created by half the population to feed the other half that cannot work. This is possible under two conditions that have limits. The first is the amount of arable land and the second the yield that can be obtained from that land.

When the number of people living off the land dropped to half the population the style economy became the predominant generator of input to the economy. This pretty much coincided with a period where the United States had the arbitrage advantage in gold and silver, the primary basis for its paper currency. Those on the land were still able to produce sufficient excess to maintain both economies. The problem that was to grow in epic proportions was that of the growth of the government sector of the economy. Instead of taking its needs from the top before distributing nature's wealth as denominated in the currency, it chose to take it back in the form of taxes. In addition, the government began assuming functions never intended in its charter that enabled it to skew the economy in favor of its supporters who allowed them to maintain that power. In order to do this it enabled banks that would collect the gold and silver used to back the currency send it to the government in exchange for paper and then put it in the hands of those who deposited it with them. The government then would selectively take back what it needed in the form of taxes. These taxes were supposed to be uniform throughout the States but never were because only those who had money could pay and those who had it were reluctant to give it up. This was partly broken up with the adoption of the sixteenth amendment to the Constitution instituting the income tax. This too was not uniform and could only be paid by those who actually had an income.

That portion of the kcal not consumed fuels the style economy and is limited. In order to augment individual holdings individuals resort to borrowing. You can only borrow what other people have saved or is surplus to their needs and available. As indicated previously, banks have been allowed to charge usury and as such are able to reintroduce kcal previously produced and saved that will not be produced until some future time and includes the usury charged by the bank. This introduces exchange into the system that is not supported by kcal production thereby decreasing the value of that exchange. Table 2 illustrates the incremental and cumulative effect on the medium of exchange as a consequence of an unbalanced economy. The books must balance each year in that production is equal to consumption and if not a change in the amount of medium must be made accordingly. When you consume more that you produce the medium's value goes down. When you produce more than you consume the value of the medium goes up. When the government guarantees deposits and loans the defaults must be made up through taxes or more borrowing that compounds the inflation. The end result it now takes about 13.01 units to purchase what 1 unit bought in 1914. That this inflationary factor has now permeated the life economy is evidenced by the fact that the price of wheat now hovers near $6.00 per bushel as opposed to $1 per bushel in 1914. Growing demand coupled with stagnant or decreasing production will insure this price will rise.

4

THE ECONOMIC HISTORY OF THE UNITED STATES

The economic history of the United States is an embarrassment of riches. Claiming ownership of land heretofore supporting the native population who embraced no concept of ownership the Kings of England, Spain and France parceled it to their favorites in exchange for taxes in order to support their regimes. As a consequence, the economic systems prevalent in these regimes were carried over to the so called "New World". The British colonies in America were no exception and the banks of the individual colonies became the intermediary in the economy enabling them to charge usury and when they didn't have actual assets to support their currencies actually printed it in anticipation that defaults would not exceed the usurious profits they could make on their loans.

These practices did not end with the Revolutionary War, only the taxes being extracted from the colonies by the British Crown. They were quietly replaced by taxes imposed by a federal government, established to replace those Congress established under the Articles of Confederation. Under the Articles the States were invoiced for their share of expenses. Some paid, others did not and the balance was made up with borrowing and the issuance of scrip or promissory notes. To eliminate this problem the first power given the new Congress under the Constitution was the power to tax to pay for the debts and expenses of the new federal government. It was means to enable a pay-as-you-go method similar to that of the States who were required to balance their budgets each year. A second power, that to borrow was included separately in order to augment taxation in the likely event of another war resulting in unusual expenses. Though it was never intended to replace the States it did not take long for the Constitution to become the blueprint of an actual government.

The first crack in the armor the framers tried to clothe the Constitution came in a dispute between Alexander Hamilton and Thomas Jefferson and William Randolph in which George Washington solicited their opinions as to the ability of the Congress to charter a National Bank. The purpose of this act was to establish an entity that would collect taxes in order to pay the debts of the United States. These debts constituted those owed the banks of France and Holland and the script issued to private U. S. citizens to finance the war, including its soldiers. Whether this scheme was an intentional fraud perpetrated by those who had bought these notes at 10 cents on the dollar will never be known but that is what happened and the purchasers were reward with redemption at full value by the National Bank.

Washington chose to accept Hamilton's opinion that the end justified the means as stipulated in his written argument, signed the act into law that was ultimately challenged but upheld in the famous case McCulloch vs. Maryland (17 US 316) of 1824. In keeping with Hamilton's original argument the court further opined, "If the end be legitimate, and within the Constitution, all the means which are appropriate, which are plainly adapted to that end, and which are not prohibited, may constitutionally be employed to carry it into effect. This decision also established the precedent that it was the Supreme Court and not the President as the party to determine the constitutionality of laws passed by the Congress. This in itself is a direct violation of the Constitution wherein this power is given to the President alone through the veto power.

THE ECONOMIC HISTORY OF THE UNITED STATES

The Bank of the United States was finally abandoned when the law lapsed and was not renewed by an administration that favored gold and silver coinage as opposed to paper. The damage was done and control of the economy returned to the State banks until 1913 when the government established the Federal Reserve System. Its original objectives were to maximize employment, stabilize prices, and moderate long-term interest rates. This was done in response to the Panic of 1907 in which uncertainty of the financial markets came about due to speculation on the country's stock markets. It has taken on other responsibilities, the major one that of regulation of the nation's banking system through the setting of internal borrowing rates between banks.

That the Constitution was more than a mutual defense pact but a skeleton on which to build a strong central government was hammered home in events leading to the Civil War. The South was an agrarian society while the North or more aptly the Northeast was a mercantile society. Unequal treatment by the Congress dominated by the Northeast due to its larger population was the primary cause of the secession movement by the southern States. The Declaration of Independence provided the license for the South to abrogate its agreement with the North. Other than the possibility the South might side with Great Britain should they decide to attack the North there was no reason the North needed the South any more than the similar threat already posed by a sparsely populated Canada to the North. The North prevailed at great cost in life but because there was still great untapped wealth in the mid-west and west not to say the gold and silver yet undiscovered financial collapse was averted by the borrowing necessary to fund the war.

Until 1900 the United States had incurred a debt of less than $1 billion, mostly as a result of the Civil War. Then we engaged in World War I in which we essentially were a mercenary army to the British and French. The Kaiser posed no threat to the United States and his only actions were to try and stop us from helping his enemies just as the attack on

Pearl Harbor was intended to stop us from helping China, Korea, the Philippines and other Pacific Nations. These were acts by legitimate governments but their objective was no different than that of today's terrorists and that is to discourage us from taking sides in disputes with their enemies or those they wished to conquer. Following the end of the war nations severely pared down their military and the western world enjoyed a period of relative prosperity. The United States ran full blast to implement the industrial revolution, fueled by its growing agricultural production while at the same time reducing its rural population who fled to the industrial heartlands to participate in the growing economy. In the period between 1915 and 1930 the economy nearly tripled. The dollar held its own because there was no deficit spending and most lending by the banks were in collateralized loans meaning the dollars were being converted into saleable fixed assets.

Just as the nation was recovering from the stock market crash of 1929 the Great Depression was ushered in with the rapid decline in agricultural production. Actions of the government to intrude in the natural evolution of a culture were to permanently change that evolution in an almost irreversible way. When the unemployed went to recover their savings from the banks they found it unavailable because the banks had loaned most of it to others resulting in many bank failures. The government stepped in to supposedly solve the problem of unemployment and financial liquidity with actions that would forever doom the U. S. economy to ultimate failure.

These actions were the National Labor Relations Act of 1935 and the Fair Labor Standards Act of 1938 and the establishment of Fannie Mae and Freddie Mac, two institutions established to buy and guarantee bank credit. The labor legislation established collective bargaining and set hours and wages, including a minimum wage for certain individuals. The banking acts that established the institutions allowed them to collateralize bank loans, primarily mortgages and guarantee their payment, thereby eliminating losses by the banks due to defaults. The labor legislation ostensibly gave unions the power to extort higher wages and benefits from employers without recourse by employers to substitute workers. Despite their being upheld by a Supreme Court populated by justices appointed by Franklin Roosevelt the Constitution does not give the Congress the power to impair the obligation of contracts and specifically prohibits the States from doing so.

World War II did not stifle this interference only exacerbated it. The impact on the economy of collective bargaining necessitated protectionism in the form of tariffs on imported goods and helped the economy for a time but it made American goods prohibitively expensive in foreign markets. Foreign countries eager to play in the dollar game could not afford the ante and American manufacturers could not play in their game when the domestic market became saturated.

The old saw you can't have your cake and eat it too is false under two conditions. The first is when you make more than you consume and the second when you can make another to replace the one you consume. It only becomes true when you have no more flour to make cake. The U. S. found itself in the former situation and to placate American manufacturers started dropping the tariffs in a series of trade agreements. Labor, unwilling to give up its gains made under collective bargaining, saw its jobs in the manufacturing sector rapidly vanish to foreign producers, particularly China. This has resulted in further government interference in the economy by taking on the role of parent, providing welfare for those who cannot work while retaining the collective bargaining advantage for government workers and those in the private sector whose jobs cannot be performed outside the country.

We have now arrived at our current condition where those still in the game and even those who have retired still want to have their cake and eat it too. This has resulted in the continuing demands of the welfare state which are growing with every addition to the population, in particular the immigrant population because when they add to the welfare demand they need everything while most existing welfare recipients can live with their parents and do not need housing, the largest single expense for most.

Even in dispensing welfare, the government is incompetent and inefficient. Welfare is no longer a hand up until its recipient can overcome the consequences of why they are on welfare. The jobs lost are not going to return until we completely abandon the current economic system and therefore welfare will be a constant and growing burden. The only beneficiaries of retraining programs and the growing welfare apparatus are the government employees who administer them. Unlike the Germans after World War I the debt cannot be paid or eliminated because it is permanent and growing. Borrowing does not replace taxation; it only further inflates the dollar.

Man's survival is inextricably connected to the land because it is the land that produces the fuel man needs to produce work because we operate an economic distribution system that requires work in order to be able to obtain the exchange necessary to purchase the fuel. This is particularly true and becomes most evident when individuals are forced or find it most convenient to steal. Groups will topple governments often through civil war when they are not given what they believe is their fair share. When an entire country reaches a point where its future is threatened because it is running out of food to feed its population it engages in war with neighbor states and slaughters and enslaves the remaining portion of its population in order to acquire land to feed its own citizens.

Table 3 shows where the nation's wealth is going. Of particular interest is the first column that shows the number of people we are feeding outside the United States. This only constitutes three of the major food staples; wheat, maize (corn) and soybeans. Domestic production is still sufficient to provide for the U. S. population but its diet is much more balanced consisting of many food items that contain lower octane, kcal if you will, and requiring more arable land for its production. As is evident from the last column, we can no longer justify the cost of adding to the latter production because since 1960 we have started importing larger and larger quantities of these fuel sources.

Table 3: Feeding the World

Data sources are the Office of Management and Budget, UN Food and Agricultural Agency (UNFAO) and the U.S. Dept. of Agriculture.

Person Equivalents @ 912,500 kcal/year

	Exports	Imports
1960	110,947,376	132,388
1970	181,032,400	2,380,169
1980	495,491,895	820,531
1990	389,533,855	6,589,114
2000	431,720,723	3,769,257
2010	518,275,390	8,329,519

The disturbing factor is that since 1922 the government has been subsidizing the production of agriculture products. Examples of such commodities include; wheat, feed grains (grain used as fodder, such as maize or corn, sorghum, barley, and oats), cotton, milk, rice, peanuts, sugar, tobacco, oilseeds such as soybeans, and meat products such as beef, pork, and lamb and mutton. This amounts to about $20 billion per year currently. These payments represent the difference between U. S. cost and the world price. You can see why agribusinesses and individual farmers would want to shift to more profitable crops and why these same businesses switch from year to year to the crops that have the highest subsidies. The ridiculousness of this policy is evident in the fact we subsidize farmers to grow corn and then subsidize the rancher who feeds it to his pigs and cattle. We have all seen the individual with a cartful of groceries that include food such as frozen lobster paying for the lot with a Supplemental Nutritional Assistance Program (SNAP) card fully funded by the federal or state government through taxes or borrowing. These abuses can only continue and get worse as the number qualifying for them increases.

Currently all U. S. production of grain staples have maxed out and it takes government subsidies to continue their production and halt the shift to more profitable production that is not subsidized by tax dollars. New immigrants whether legal or illegal are being housed and clothed as well as fed by tax dollars. In addition, government workers, including those whose jobs are totally dependent on government are paid for with tax dollars. All those retired and collecting social security or other government welfare payments are being subsidized with tax dollars because even those who contributed to Social Security had their payments already spent and are therefore being subsidized with current tax dollars.

Production of wheat in the United States hit is peak in 1979 and has been on a downward trend ever since. It is down nearly 30% from its peak. Corn reached its peak in 2003 and has been in steady decline albeit more slowly because its subsidy is higher due to its use to produce ethanol. The problem being created or should I say is being exacerbated is production of the most efficient kcal producers is dropping, the number of people being supported in whole or in part by government subsidies is increasing. The population is also increasing and most of these new entrants do not have family or private charity to fall back on and the result more of them require assistance.

Compounding this problem are countries, primarily China who are now arbitraging the U. S. dollar due to the trade imbalance in the style economy. The Chinese trade differential now exceeds $365 billion dollars yearly. China's largest purchases from the United States are agricultural products including wheat, rice, soybeans and sorghum. Unlike the United States, China does not grow enough food to feed its population and must not only import but subsidize its own rice and wheat producers to keep them like the United States from shifting to more profitable crops. Their ability to arbitrage the U. S. dollar essentially means they can buy our treasury notes and food products with our own money. It is why our State Department has been trying to pressure the Chinese to adjust the value of their currency against the dollar. The problem is they did just that but in the other direction, devaluing the Yuan against the dollar. Other countries, in particular Japan have done this in order to protect their export industries.

There is nothing manufactured in the United States than cannot be manufactured in China if it chose to do so. Because of its ability to arbitrage the U. S. dollar it chooses not to manufacture such items as commercial aircraft and expensive medical diagnostic equipment because it is cheaper to buy them from the likes of Boeing and General Electric while at the same time placating U. S. trade negotiators who further erode the U.S. labor market when implementing trade agreements like the North American Free Trade Agreement and the most recent Pacific Trade Pact. The United States is no longer the world's leading industrial power. Only our agriculture surpasses that of any other country in producing a surplus that we are rapidly frittering away. When we sell subsidized wheat to buy oranges it is like selling money at a discount.

Summary

The U. S. dollar is backed by the full faith and credit of the United States. That credit is based on the kcal of the food we produce in excess of our own population's requirements. That production has already reached its maximum and we are already importing some of our needs. A growing portion of the population obtains those kcal through government subsidized work or charity, whether private or government. If you do not work you do not eat unless someone with a surplus shares with you. The U. S. government, better the people it represents, must take from those who work a certain portion of their income in order to be charitable because voluntary contributions, or private charity, are insufficient to meet the needs of the growing number of people who do not or cannot work.

To placate those who work and pay taxes to support those who do not work the government pays or forces private enterprise to pay increased wages and salaries to their employees. When it fails to tax to meet these obligations government borrows the difference, inflating the value of the currency. Because of this inflation, individuals no longer save so the money being used to purchase government bonds or notes is money that has already been spent thereby causing further inflation. When foreign banks purchase these securities with their dollar reserves they are actually using dollars that have already been converted to their own currency. The United States Treasury is in essence taking out a mortgage on what supports the economy, its agricultural production.

We have now reached a point where the U. S. government has taken on obligations for future expenses, primarily welfare and pensions that cannot be sustained with the present level of taxation. They certainly cannot when these expenditures continue to rise. We are already like Greece, where those receiving benefits from the government in the form of salaries or pensions refuse to relinquish them in order to stabilize income and expenditure without borrowing. In the United States we have reached that point and we are borrowing from ourselves and others to sustain an economy that is unsustainable and in the process deflating our currency even faster. Unlike Germany, we cannot cancel the debt or go bankrupt because our debt is the very lives of our citizens.

There is a better way.

5

THE KCAL ECONOMY

The United Nations Food and Agriculture Organization (UNFAO) keeps tabs on the world's food supply and maintains statistics on the production, import and export of nearly all agricultural commodities. The reliability of these statistics is only as good as the government organizations that provide them but, from a macro point of view, they are sufficiently accurate to indicate trends and potential problems such as malnutrition. They have been used extensively in the preparation of this paper.

It has been posited that grains are the most efficient food sources because they provide not only the kcal fuel requirements of populations but, the nutritional variety to sustain good health. A country is fortunate if it can produce commodities such as wheat, corn, soybeans and rice in sufficient quantity to sustain their population and as well have sufficient arable land to produce tubers, vegetables and fruit as an adjunct or substitute for an all grain diet. Very few countries have this abundance and many must import a large portion of their food supply. Of the latter, the ability to import is totally dependent on whether they have other goods or commodities in the style economy in competition with others in a similar situation.

The basis of determination of adequacy of a nation's food supply is the ability to produce sufficient kcal to sustain the population. Every food source has kcal content the amount of which can be determined by analysis. For example; wheat has a kcal value of 327 per 100 grams. Corn has 365, cane sugar 550 and soybeans 446 per 100g. Production, export and import figures supplied by the UNFAO are given in metric tons so the number of kcal per metric ton is a very large number that I have reduced to a human equivalent by assuming the average person needs 2500 kcal per day or 912,500 kcal per year. The resultant index for each commodity is the number of average individuals each metric ton will support for one year until the next growing cycle. They are; wheat 3.64/mton, corn 4.07/mton, rice 4.07/mton and soybeans 4.97/mton.

In terms of food, the United States is the richest country in the world. How rich? We only need examine its recent production of the commodities I have chosen to represent the most efficient usage of arable land. In 2014 the United States produced 55.4 million metric tons of wheat, 10 million metric tons of rice, 361 million metric tons of corn and 108 million metric tons of soybeans. Based on a nearly 1 million kcal annual diet this is enough kcal to feed nearly 2.25 billion people. This does not include many other food commodities produced all of which are being consumed by someone or something every year and yet there are people going hungry or malnourished in the United States each year despite government welfare.

The answer to this dichotomy is in the manner of distribution of this wealth of nature. Much of the corn is used to feed animals and fowl for human consumption. Much of it is exported, particularly wheat and corn to places where there is insufficient domestic production such as the oil rich countries like Kuwait, Saudi Arabia, the United Arab Emirates and Qatar. Mexico for example produces only enough of the aforementioned commodities to provide for only 110 million of its over 125 million population. It uses a large amount of its arable land to grow low kcal but high labor content foods such as fruits and vegetables to export to the United States in order to buy wheat and corn to supplement its kcal needs. Because much of what is available is unequally distributed a large number of those on the short end are migrating to the United States illegally where they can participate in obtaining some of the large U.S. surplus.

THE KCAL ECONOMY

The Unites States does not have a surplus per se because every kcal produced is consumed albeit by people in other countries. Being overlooked is the fact that little if no arable land has been converted to additional food production since the 1980s and more is being taken out or converted to commodities that provide greater profit to its producers. Nowhere is this situation more evident than in central Africa and non-oil rich countries of the Middle East such as Syria. Syria produces just 2 million metric tons of wheat, enough to feed only 7.3 million of its 26 million population. Granted it does grow other commodities that make up some of the difference and imports enough to sate the needs of those who support the government that determines the distribution. Those who come up short have been leaving and the remainder is now organized to fight to change the distribution. This latter situation is becoming more commonplace as more and more countries are faced with the dilemma of more mouths to feed than resources to feed them.

A system that requires one to work in order to survive will itself not survive because it ignores the fact that not everyone can work such as the youth, the infirm and the elderly who cannot compete for what few jobs there are requiring human intervention. We have overlooked the fact that when we employ a machine that can produce ten or a hundred times more than a single individual we have eliminated nine and ninety nine individuals from the opportunity to earn a living.

Only a kcal economic system that provides every individual with the exchange necessary to purchase the time of others who provide what one cannot provide for oneself represents a fair distribution of nature's wealth. It recognizes that each individual is not significantly different as regards the requirement for food as fuel yet enables those who utilize that fuel to provide for the needs and wants of his fellow man to enjoy a better lifestyle. Such a system is self-governing and only requires that any government needed is solely constituted to protect the lives, liberties and property of its adherents by preventing and punishing theft.

6

THE REAL ECONOMY

Free Market Capitalism is an economic system that rewards success, punishes failure and theft while allowing maximum freedom of association. Its only law is you shall not steal and its only regulations, which are applicable to everyone equally, are those which protect the lives, the liberties and the property of its participants. It acknowledges the gains and losses from investment but disallows the gains and losses of speculation. The investment of money in a business to provide a good or service for the purpose of making a profit is the essence of free market capitalism. Making money on money through speculation such as usury in its original form, gambling or betting on the vagaries of stocks, bonds and other commercial paper is unacceptable. The system is governed by representatives of the people whose only task is to define theft, apprehend and punish those who do and to make those regulations necessary for the protection of the lives, liberties and property of its participants as well as those unable. It is the police power that members surrender in part when forming a society in order to protect that society.

The capitalist system works on the basis of value added and acknowledges that all things go through a process of depletion or depreciation, including humans. The system has the following basic tenets:

1. Limitation of membership to that which can be sustained by the renewable assets of nature under the society's control.
2. The land and its assets belong to the people and the society

THE REAL ECONOMY

they have established to govern themselves. Its loan to individuals and the conditions of its use is to be determined by the government selected by the citizens.

3. Parents are responsible for the education of their children who, in order to become citizens must achieve a minimum proficiency in reading, writing and basic mathematics as determined by the citizenry. Parents are allocated their children's distribution until such time as they reach this proficiency

4. Competition insures that goods and services are available at the lowest cost to those who want them.

5. The value of one's labor is determined by what a consumer is willing and able to pay the producer.

6. The value of a product is the sum total of the value of its component parts.

7. The price of a product is equal to its value when supply equals demand.

8. The price of a product is whatever amount a willing seller will accept and a willing buyer pay.

9. Subsequent sale of goods above its value is deemed unearned income and any amount gained in this manner is taxed at 100% unless its value has been enhanced.

10. The unit of exchange shall be the N$ and shall be issued in such form as appropriate on the basis of N$=2500kcal per citizen per day. It shall be distributed by a government agency responsible directly to the people or their representatives and that shall be responsible for the collection and accuracy of the production of adequate food staples that support the currency. The distribution shall be in equal amounts at appropriate times to each citizen to whose account it shall be credited. Rules for the operation of the agency and compensation of its employees shall be as determined by the citizens or their representatives.

11. Theft is the only law that shall be punished by other than fines and its commission will be appropriately punished up to and including being declared wards of the state. A ward of the state is anyone who cannot fend for himself in the society without assistance. They will be cared for in facilities funded and staffed by the state with the funds available from their share of the distribution. Any law proposed must obtain at minimum the consent of 90% of the body chosen to approve it. Any law may be subsequently repealed or amended but no law shall be passed that makes any form of theft permissible.

12. No law or regulation shall be imposed that makes illegal anything heretofore not deemed illegal or regulated. There can be no ex post facto laws. For example, a society cannot ban or regulate the use or consumption of anything naturally occurring or that can be made from such material.

13. All laws and regulations shall be applicable to everyone and no law or regulation shall be imposed that gives benefit or punishment to any individual or group. Such so called "bills of attainder" are specifically prohibited.

14. Regulations are rules of conduct to protect the lives, liberties and property of the citizens the lack of adherence to them shall be punished by fines. Any regulation proposed must obtain the consent of at least 90% of those chosen to approve them. Regulations may be modified or eliminated by a vote of 51% if they fail to achieve the objective intended. The first decision to be made for a proposed action is whether there is a need for action or not. If a majority (51%) says there is a need the next thing to debate is how to implement that action. A vote on any course is not sufficient since 49% may have said there was no need in the first instance. Therefore you need not only convince all 51% who thought that action was needed but 51% of those who thought no action was needed. If you cannot, then no action is taken. This alternative is often ignored in any

decision process and why compromise rarely works.

15. All those charged with breaking the law or not adhering to any regulation shall be considered guilty unless they can prove their innocence in which case they will be appropriately compensated. Nowhere in the U. S. Constitution or that of any of the several states is it stipulated that a person is innocent until proven guilty. It is easier to prove innocence than guilt and the current system is a contrivance of politicians who are primarily lawyers for their own aggrandizement.

16. A government is established by the citizens such as to make and administer the laws and regulations necessary to carry out these tenets. No law shall be passed that permits or encourages theft or allows it to go unpunished and anyone who attempts or participates in passage of such law shall be forever barred from holding public office or government employment. No regulations shall be imposed that inhibit the free exercise of individual rights except those necessary to protect life, liberty and property and any licenses issued to individuals or associations of individuals shall contain a proviso such as to control the discharge of waste or material into the environment that can be proven to be harmful to life, liberty or property.

17. A separate and independent judiciary shall be established to hear disputes between citizens, between citizens and government and whose members shall be selected by the citizenry from among their peers.

18. Government serves at the pleasure of the citizenry and citizens have a right to challenge the actions of anyone in government and their complaint shall take precedence over other actions of government. Frivolous actions are to be discouraged and those that are found unsupported severely punished by fines.

19. Any utility deemed necessary for public funding such as electricity generation, water purification, sewage and waste disposal may have its initial capital investment funded through

voluntary deductions from government disbursement. Ultimate operations and maintenance, including the escrow of such funds necessary to recover the initial capital investment shall be paid for only by the users through rates, tolls or license fees.

Society's Membership

It was Thomas Malthus, in the eighteenth century, who foresaw the ultimate demise of man as being related to overpopulation. The earth's resources are finite and it requires air, water, food and light to sustain life. When any of these is no longer available life will perish. Nature has a process called photosynthesis that allows plant life to utilize the carbon dioxide in the atmosphere combined with light, minerals in the earth and water to reproduce itself and to produce oxygen necessary for the sustenance of animal life. The carbon dioxide is replenished by burning caused by natural fires or the acts of man in the burning of fossil fuels.

It does not seem possible that when God commanded Moses to "go forth and multiply" that He meant exponentially. Nevertheless, that is almost exactly what has happened. Only the ingenuity of man has been able to exact the maximum out of the arable land available to supply the food necessary for the growing population. On the negative side are the actions of man that exacerbate the growing problem of feeding the ever growing population. These are:

1. Discouraging the formation of producers while at the same time encouraging the formation of consumers.

2. Erection of borders both physical and legal to prevent migration and restrict trade.

3. Unequal distribution of wealth by manipulation of the currency of exchange.

THE REAL ECONOMY

There are three ways to survive in this world; you can earn it, you can share in the surplus afforded others or you can steal it from them. The only law that is necessary to sustain the life nature provides is you shall not steal. There is no surplus food. It is either consumed by the society that produces it, sold to other societies or goes to waste and only so much is produced each year. Each person, on average, consumes 2500 kcal per day. An individual will have to earn 2500 kcal per day continuously and to feed a family of four it will require 10,000 kcal per day.

As Malthus surmised, his government in order to control its ever increasing British population did two things that made matters worse instead of better. They forced primogeniture and poor taxes on producers and gave subsidies to consumers. Primogeniture gave the right to the eldest son to inherit the wealth of the father leaving any additional sons in the ranks of consumers unless they can fend on their own without a head start. In addition there was the poor tax which enabled the subsidy to the poor to buy the food for their survival. The common rule is that if you want to discourage something you tax it and if you want to encourage it you subsidize it. It applies to the production of children as well as any other perceived abuses that should be tempered by the self-control encouraged by the free market capitalist economic system. Self-governance is the first line of defense of any society.

In a land as rich in nature's wealth as the United States the formation of families is not only encouraged but made possible by the availability of these riches. The problem is that we have become a society whose objective is the uneven distribution of this wealth on a basis not determined by the value of the contribution of the society's producers. Such a society cannot survive and collect a greater share of this wealth unless they take control of government and eliminate rules and regulations that make the family dependent on the charity of government rather than its own human capital. The U. S. dollar is backed by the full faith and credit of the United States. That credit is based on the kcal of the food we produce in excess of our own population's requirements.

A society has a right, if not an obligation, to control its membership to that which it can support and to ensure its support is adequate to weather calamities that may befall it. The old rules of licensing on condition that close relations or people with transmittable venereal disease should not be licensed to reproduce was adequate and those who do so without license should not be rewarded for their failure to comply with society's rules. If this is not sufficient to maintain society's numbers, they can be augmented by applicants from other societies.

It is the epitome of self-governance to recognize that one should not bring into this world a soul that cannot be self-supporting. Pregnancy can be avoided if not eliminated by self-control. Society, if it is to share in nature's blessing, must also recognize it must share in nature's anomalies such as multiple births, Siamese twins and birth defects. When these are the consequence of unlicensed pairings society has an obligation to itself to see that the miscreants are not rewarded but punished and take whatever action appropriate under the circumstances to see to it that the child is not punished as well.

Self-control is enhanced by the penalties incurred due to the lack of it. Deadbeat dads, for example, that father children without license can be automatically punished financially by withholding a portion of their distribution. The mother likewise and the child made a ward of the state until such time as they can be placed in a home of those who have been unsuccessful in having children or in a foster home. The economic system put forward will restore the family to its rightful place in society and encourage self-governance as regards reproduction.

The Distribution

The key to a free market economy is the distribution of nature's wealth in the form of exchange tied to a society's ability to feed it people. This includes children and the elderly who, because of competition, cannot work but require subsistence. It also includes those with physical and mental disabilities. If each is entitled to 912,500 kcal for each year of their lives there is no need for them to work just to survive. A natural limit on the amount any one individual can obtain by working makes each individual able to pay for the services needed and with a modicum of savings able to bridge unforeseen expenses making insurance and saving for retirement redundant.

The Land

The land and the people are inextricably linked because it is the land and the bounty of food that sustain life and produce the human effort necessary to maintain it. It is also the source of non-reproducible elements that fuel the style economy. The land belongs to all earth's inhabitants and each individual, family, tribe, state and country is responsible for its care and custody for whatever time they can defend it from theft by others. The only obligation these societal units have is to insure that portion of the land over which they claim jurisdiction can provide sufficient food to support its members. The society then has the obligation to govern itself in such a way as to allocate the appropriate amount of land to agriculture, habitation and industry in that order of priority and put in place a free market economic system that insures that participants in each phase of the economy are rewarded with the same priority. The free market capitalist model is that economic system and Republicanism is the manner in which it is implemented.

Most countries base their diets on two major food groups headed by wheat or rice. Based on average yields, wheat produces 33.4 million kcal per acre and rice 22 million kcal per acre though as many as three crops of rice can be grown. The major reason for growing rice as opposed to wheat is geography the condition of the terrain and the abundance of water. Rice is grown in paddies and sloped land is more conducive to rice growing than wheat, which benefits from a flatter terrain and far less manpower. Paddies maximize use of water whether irrigation or rain. Fortunately the United States has plenty of rice and wheat and is a major exporter of both commodities.

The dollar is the reserve currency of most countries with the exception of China because the United States has been the world's largest style economy until recently. It is why the worlds traded commodities are priced in US Dollars. The difference is that neither those countries on a wheat based economy nor those on a rice based economy measure their currency in kcal. They distribute their wealth in a non-uniform manner or base it on actual produced wealth. The $ has been allowed to "float" that is its measure is based on comparison to the purchasing power of other world currencies. I have posited that this predominant position is because the U. S. produces more kcal than any other country and is the real backing behind the $. In a kcal based economy the books must balance at the end of each year (growing season) because what is produced is consumed or saved in some form, there is no surplus. What cannot be sold (distributed) rots or goes to waste including a portion that is sold. The United States is already $18 trillion in debt which means it has already spent the output and consumption for generations yet unborn. In 2005 the U. S. exported $62 billion in surplus agricultural products. If that income were used to pay the debt it would take 274 years to pay it off.

Following World War II the Bretton Woods Conference of world bankers and governments set the pattern for world trade after the disruptions caused by the war. The gold standard was changed and the value of gold set at $35/oz. double its market value in 1914. Any arbitrage left had long since disappeared. The United States was subsidizing the gold and silver producers because it needed gold and silver for coinage. This meant you could go to any bank in the United States and for $35 in notes change it into gold to use in world trade. This lasted until 1968 when government inflationary policies, particularly in the United States, raised the cost of production of gold above its imputed value in dollars. This value was enhanced by the higher cost of labor resulting from federal labor legislation. Gold and other precious metals or minerals have been used as a proxy for food to no avail because they lack reproducibility are of limited supply and therefore not of constant value. What better commodity to use than food itself and its constant value the kcal.

Most Populous Countries kcal Factor

Table 4 illustrates the agriculture production of the world's most populous countries as regards the commodities wheat, rice, corn and soybeans in relation to the kcal available to each citizen, a factor of 1.0 being the equivalent of 912,500 kcal per year or 2500 kcal per day. The factor has been developed from the metric tons produced in 2013 as obtained from the UNFAO FAOSTAT data series and converting this production to kcal equivalents and dividing the result by 912,500 for each member of the 2013 population. Each must be looked at individually as to whether this seeming shortfall in self-sufficiency because of two factors; the ability to import its needs and the sufficiency of alternatives. Japan for example is a rice based economy and its style economy produces sufficient export revenue to procure any shortfall on the world market. It also has a sophisticated welfare system that insures distribution reaches the vast majority of its citizens. Nigeria on the other hand is an oil rich country and can afford to import any shortfall in its domestic food requirements. It does not have an elaborate welfare system and the distribution favors those who run the country and those who support them. As a consequence, minority tribes are constantly at war with the entrenched powers to wrest that power away. Prior to organized upheaval is migration that is the case with Mexico. It is also evident why the Soviet Union wants to annex part of the Ukraine.

This snapshot does not tell the full story. It can be reversed and the shortfalls corrected by more efficient use of arable land, the expansion of arable land and improvements in irrigation. The problem is just the reverse is true and even where the problems have been recognized the corrections are not keeping pace with increase in need. The UNFAO has been warning against these problems for years without success because most countries do not see beyond the immediate horizon. The danger is of course in the trends and none of them are good but the leadership of the world does not want to take the steps necessary the first of which is that there is a problem.

The United States currently enjoys a considerable advantage yet we have people who do not get enough to eat and others whose lifestyle is less than it could be if there was a better distribution. In addition, we have considerable tracts of land that could be adapted to cultivation if needed. The emphasis by those who control the distribution is not the welfare of the people they control but, themselves and those who put them in positions of power and keep them there. The latter can definitely be changed with an implementation of free market capitalism and Republicanism.

	Pop. Mil.	kcal Factor		Pop. Mil.	kcal Factor		Pop. Mil.	kcal Factor
China	1,362	1.87	Germany	81	1.61	Kenya	44	0.39
India	1,238	1.03	Iran	77	0.95	Argentina	40	12.46
USA	317	7.63	Turkey	76	1.31	Poland	39	1.09
Indonesia	250	1.70	Congo	68	0.12	Algeria	38	0.31
Brazil	201	2.75	Thailand	66	2.68	Sudan	38	0.00
Pakistan	185	0.99	France	66	3.86	Canada	35	5.59
Nigeria	173	0.41	UK	64	1.09	Iraq	34	3.80
Banglades	153	1.72	Italy	60	0.63	Morocco	33	0.83
Russia	144	1.82	Burma	53	2.80	Uzbekista	30	0.99
Japan	127	0.34	S. Africa	53	1.26	Saudi Ara	30	0.18
Mexico	118	0.90	S. Korea	50	0.64	Malaysia	30	0.46
Phillipines	99	1.22	Columbi	47	0.22	Venezuela	29	6.24
Vietnam	90	2.41	Spain	47	0.67	Afghanist	26	1.03
Ethiopia	87	0.45	Ukraine	45	5.17			
Egypt	84	0.80	Tanzania	45	0.00	World	7,200	1.81

Table 4 – Country kcals

Land is not arable without water and it is water that is unevenly distributed throughout the planet. This has not stopped the development of irrigation systems to maximize the efficiency or earth's natural purifications system, evaporation into the atmosphere and rain, much of which goes to waste when it falls back into the oceans. This effort has been driven by the increase in population which is hastening the demise of life on earth. Ownership of the land gives its owner the opportunity to share nature's bounty but also gives him the opportunity to deny it. It is the responsibility of society to see to it that no individual or group can control what the land produces and those who have stewardship over the land and what it produces are suitably compensated for their efforts and that they do so indiscriminately.

In the 1960s we embarked on a program to put a man on the moon and after nearly 10 years and $1 trillion we succeeded. Money and human effort could have been better spent on a more productive and lasting effort by harnessing our rivers, building dams and irrigation facilities. It would have provided renewable power, more food production and alleviated the devastation caused by floods.

An observation of our known universe should provide a clue that life on earth will ultimately come to an end and it will be because one of the elements necessary for life will be exhausted. It is only a matter of when. Parts of the world are already overpopulated and it has only been the ingenuity of man in supplementing nature that has enabled those here to survive. It has also been man who has chosen those of his society who should get more or less from an ever dwindling pot. Conversion to a free market capitalist system would correct these inequities.

Education

Education is the development of knowledge, skill and character. In an agrarian and mercantile economy the fundamentals were learned in the home or religious center and the children then learned what was necessary at the feet of their parents and took up their trade or occupation. The religious center was important because in it they had their knowledge of right and wrong reinforced and more importantly its commonality among the society of their peers. It also exposed them to the knowledge and abilities of others in the community the key being to learn the language and accumulate a vocabulary and know-how to construct and understand the meaning of sentences. Basically it is the building of vocabulary and how to employ it to convey understanding and meaning. Technology has greatly increased the vocabulary but at the same time expanded its reach and availability to where it can now be acquired by more people faster than ever before. It now seems wasteful to dole it out in proscribed lots over a long period of time therefore making the public school system fashioned in the days of limited communication obsolete. Knowledge is now everywhere for the taking and all that is necessary is the realization that knowledge is not only necessary for survival but the key to the quality of life and who but the parents to demonstrate this truth and instill it in their progeny.

Deists invented the public school system in the United States as a replacement for the education received in the church without the dogma and religious teaching and made it mandatory. The new religion is progressivism that teaches government has all the answers and metes out favors and punishment to those in its charge. It is the single most causal factor in the breaking down of the bonds of family, aside from the economic system. Government had no charter from society for this purpose and parents should be free to educate their children in any manner they wish as a matter of personal freedom. They are responsible for their children's actions and will be given the child's share of nature's bounty until such time they can demonstrate they are capable of fending on their own in society. Society's only obligation is to establish the standards, means and timing of a determination and the child or the parents may petition for an evaluation as often as requested or until such time the parents determine the child incapable of self-sufficiency. If, and when, the parents consider themselves no longer capable of caring for the health and welfare of their dependent offspring they may petition for them to become wards of society.

Competition

The first man who produces something people either need or want has a monopoly on the sale of that something. He has two choices; he can make a windfall by charging whatever the market will bear until a competitor enters the market and forces prices down or, he can price his product or service low enough to discourage competitors from entering the market. The latter strategy works until the cost of delivery to farther distant markets ultimately entices a competitor to enter the market. It is a self-correcting system even in the event of collusion. When all producers collude to increase prices the free market capitalism rules are invoked where increases beyond the lowest price charged is taxed away and penalties applied as the action is deemed to be theft, no value having been added to justify the price increase.

Patents and copyrights were designed to afford a means to reward intellectual capital and were a carryover from the British system which served as the model for U. S. Constitutions. The efficacy of a system that affords inventors and author's monopoly rights is highly questionable because the real reward is the ability to be first into the market and the lowest cost producer and giving a monopoly denies the public the opportunity to fulfill their needs or wants at the lowest cost. Policing such a system is next to impossible as we have quickly learned when rip-offs are nearly impossible to detect. The only ones who make anything from patent or copyright disputes are lawyers and from both the winners and losers.

The Price of Labor

Two factors inherent in Republicanism determine the compensation for human effort in both the life and style economies. They are the limit on the amount of exchange and competition. The limit on the amount of exchange and hence the distribution depend on the agricultural output basis of the economy. In the case of the United States I have suggested grains because in the end if we do not produce enough grain or something we can trade for it our society will die. Competition and the elimination of advantage of monopoly determine that the maximum one can charge for his services is the same as he obtains from the distribution under the kcal economic system.

The latter may be hard to comprehend but the fact is that with competition anyone trying to sell himself for twice the distribution will entice others, earning nothing to develop the skill necessary to drive down the price. In addition, those claiming more will be faced with employer decisions as to whether they can recover the cost from the market whose total volume is limited to the total distribution.

Labor costs have been out of control since the enactment of the National Labor Relations and Fair Labor Standards Acts and the imposition of not a maximum wage but a minimum one. Such a policy is ridiculous because some people will actually work for free. If you doubt it, the entire private welfare system depends on the existence of people who will give of their time without compensation. Not even our unfair tax systems give credit for that.

What the minimum wage has done is overprice all labor by giving a decided advantage to those who can extort money from their employer while not simultaneously increasing their salable output. At first the United States was able to protect this practice with tariffs which denied foreign producers access to U. S. markets and the dollars they could earn to procure U. S. products they could not obtain elsewhere. To placate U. S. companies who wanted these markets for their surplus production the tariffs were dropped driving the protected firms to flee overseas, if they could, or flooded the U. S. market with goods produced in countries with lesser paid workers.

This of course begs the question; will U. S. workers ever work for the same wages as foreign workers if a new economic system is imposed? The answer to that is an obvious no, not as long as the U. S. government is paying people through welfare payments not to work. It is not so much that they are being paid not to work as it is being paid not to steal, because the government is stealing for them by taxing those who work and printing money backed by IOUs.

The minimum wage is the distribution. Anything above that increases the lifestyle of the worker because his survival is guaranteed by the distribution. He will work for the same wage as that of the Chinese or Indian worker because the minimum for which he must work is the distribution the U. S. worker gets without working and he too must work at something or spend most of his distribution buying his needs and wants from others.

Employment

Having posited that an unencumbered free market is the only system that can implement Republicanism it is necessary to establish how that system will work. The initial distribution of exchange initiates the system and is its driving force. An individual, if he is prepared to perform all the activities necessary to bring his allotment of kcal to his table can retain all of his exchange to use for other purposes or enhance his style of life by joining the workforce. It has been shown that the former is next to impossible because the actual kcals are in the custody of others and as a consequence every individual must have someone else providing them for him.

The desire to work is driven by need and want. The need is to obtain food, water and air to sustain life and the want to enhance ones style of life beyond mere existence. The opportunity is created by the fact that others have those same needs and wants and like everyone else have the wherewithal to pay for what they cannot obtain on their own. Those opportunities can only exist if there is sufficient demand for them and these demands are filled in a competitive market place. Based on the amount of the annual distribution in our system all the exchange distributed is spent or saved by its recipients.

We know from experience that there is no such thing as full employment since only machines are capable of constant and sustained effort on a continuous basis and even they require time for maintenance and need fuel only when they are working. A full time job, particularly those requiring additional physical effort cannot be performed on a sustained basis and requires additional rest. Most jobs are part time if only to the extent that they entail presence but no effort. In addition many jobs, particularly in basic agriculture and construction are seasonal. More still are temporary and geographically dependent. Under Republicanism and a fixed market determined by kcal production demand will not exceed supply and that full employment is not only impractical but impossible and competition will insure this to be true.

It has been shown that the economy is fixed at the amount of the distribution and the number of persons competing for it variable. The average N$ distribution among those competing is therefore the distribution divided by the number of competitors. No single competitor can satisfy all of the needs and wants of the society but their compensation can never exceed twice that of the average. If such an anomaly occurs a competitor earning less would either offer to perform the task for less, attain the additional skill necessary and offer to do the task for less, or the free market would reject absorption of the higher cost and seek alternatives or do without. Under a free market economy monopoly practices result in taxation at 100% of all gains above the lowest price charged. The economy under Republicanism is therefore self-policing and self-correcting.

Anatomy of a Job and Human Capital

Every job has five facets; sales and marketing, acquisition of raw materials, processing or production, finance and administration and delivery. As an organization grows from a single entrepreneur, through a partnership, limited liability company and corporation the division of labor becomes more pronounced and begins to take on an identity of its own. Each requires a different level and type of preparation, skill acquisition and performance culminating in the acquisition of human capital that enhances the compensation paid for its application.

Humans working together as a team are not constrained by numbers but by the process itself. Henry Ford demonstrated that higher efficieincies can be obtained by bringing the work to the worker rather than having the workers obtain it individually. One of their numbers is chosen to perform the facilitating function relieving the others from that portion of work that is only supportive of the task or process to be performed and the abilities of the individuals performing it.

Supervision has the connotation that individuals need to be watched in order to perform and I have experienced the reverse. If, as they are capable after training to perform certain functions and will do so in order to retain their job, employees do not need supervision but facilitation in order to perform as expected. Prior to government interference in the labor market an employee performed what they were hired to do for fear of being replaced by someone who would. Unions, in particular, have removed that fear to the extent that an employer now avoids discharging an employee for fear of reprisal by labor courts biased in favor of labor.

When the number of people doing the job exceeds one it falls to at least one to perform the ancillary tasks necessary to sustain the process. Say they are engaged in a process. They are both more efficient if one obtains the raw material and takes away the finished product than if they both perform all functions independently. This sequence continues until one is occupied full time in facilitating the work of the others. This individual, usually the acknowledged leader of the group is then responsible for training replacements and assessing performance of the crew as well as performing the ancillary functions of raw material acquisition, sales, administration and finance.

Leaders are neither born nor made, they evolve. The characteristics of leadership are capability of superior performance, tempered by the desire to set a pace the others are able to maintain and humility in not flaunting one's capability to outperform. A leader helps the newcomer to reach the norm of the group and shares the credit for the group's achievements. He demonstrates his ability for upward mobility by working closely with those who help facilitate the work of the group and cooperates with those who add further value to their output. It has been my experience that an astute employer will acknowledge that the group itself selects their leader and allows the group to decide whether newcomers fit or not. I have found this system to work exceptionally well in foreign countries where ownership and labor work more collaboratively for their mutual interests and government does not cause friction by favoring one or the other.

This is basically the evolution of the small entrepreneurial business in our economy and constitutes its largest portion. Many fail because the entrepreneur has failed to acquire the ancillary skills outside the process. In this case a partnership may keep the business afloat and even allow it to grow if the market is not saturated. Saturation under Republicanism occurs when the demand for goods and services consumes the entire distribution and there is nothing being saved.

When a business expands to a point where more capital is needed than is available from its founders or the founders wish to share the risk of large capital investment they take the company public through the issuance of share ownership represented by stock. The sale of such stock is offered by a prospectus that in words and figures attempts to convince prospective investors that the business is viable and will return a profit on their investment. The sellers have supposedly tested the market to gauge demand, estimated the costs of sales, production and distribution and have priced the output such that a profit will ensue. They will have named a board of directors to guide the company's future and oversee operations to the extent they conform to the claims of the prospectus. Part of the promise is the existence of sufficient working capital until sales and income is sufficient to pay the current bills, labor being the first required by law.

All is well and good if the company meets or exceeds the expectations laid out in the prospectus. The first sign is a decline or absence of anticipated profits. The board of directors is then called upon to ascertain the reasons and institute corrections if possible. If the corrections fail the first sign will be a reduction in working capital which at that point means the income is insufficient to cover the obligations and the firm is technically bankrupt. Neither labor nor ownership is at risk because whatever they are paid is extra to the distribution but the investment of the shareholders is at risk because they will ultimately lose their investment.

The reasons for corporate failures are many but boil down to one and that is the inability to recover the cost of production. When that failure is due to internal labor cost reorganization and downsizing may provide some relief but in the end it is the market that determines the health and ultimately the fate of any corporation.

On the up side, if the market was properly estimated and costs adequately covered the shareholders are rewarded with a return on their investment. The problem then becomes one of keeping labor and management from stealing it. When the prospectus was first produced to entice investors its supporting documentation contained the organization chart, staffing plans and estimated salaries and wages to be paid that would have to be recouped from sales. If the staffing was achieved at or near the estimates the corporation is under no obligation to pay labor and management staff at any higher level unless it is accompanied by an increase in saleable output. Since sales can go either way any short term increases are best rewarded by bonuses rather than payroll increases for the simple reason if the personnel can be acquired and retained at free market rates, there is no justification for denying investors the return on their investment.

The bylaws under which the board operates in overseeing the activities of the company under economic rules of Republicanism dictate that the shareholders are the ones entitled to profits of the enterprise before any other distribution is made. The incentive to maintain this is reinforced by the free market rule that the value of ownership to the investor is determined by the dividend and not on the increase in value of the stock because if it is sold the difference from what was paid and the selling price is either taken as a loss or taxed away. The board may recommend a bonus if profits exceed expectations as a means to retain or reward contributing employees but it is up to the shareholders to approve or amend such recommendations.

Assume you want a lounge chair and you find the one you want in two different mail order catalogs. They are identical and from the same original manufacturer except one is fully assembled and the other some assembly but with a set of assembly instructions. Whether you are working to earn a better standard of living or not your time has value because if you do it yourself you will be able to retain a portion of the distribution to spend on other things. It has been shown that in a free market that unless you cannot or somehow are prohibited from doing so you should do it yourself if the time it would take you more than twice that of someone you could hire to do it for you. In this manner, the free market is self-correcting in that if obstacles appear that restrict an individual's ability to acquire skills and create a monopoly competition will appear to offset the monopoly gains.

THE REAL ECONOMY

There are two major types of jobs; one requiring both physical and mental acumen and one requiring mental acumen alone. The first requires the manipulation of tools and machinery and the second does not. The manipulation of calculators and computers and sophisticated measuring devices do not distinguish between the two as they are now common to both. Both require an elementary education to the level of understanding the language and the ability to communicate both orally and in writing. Non-physical tasks require a formal education preferably with concentration on the specific field one wishes to pursue. The additional education primarily focusses on the language peculiar to a profession and the context in which it is used. You may recall that German and Latin were prerequisites to the professions of science and medicine respectively because most of the texts used to teach these subjects were in those languages. American progress in both these fields has replaced this need and the reverse now seems to be the norm.

Formal, informal or on the job training requires a sacrifice in earnings and is often accompanied by additional cost that can only be recouped if the attainment of an entry level job is the result. As is too often discovered, the time and money one spends attaining additional education is not always rewarded with a job opportunity in the field of one's choice, particularly if it is needed to earn a living. Republicanism and a free market economy remove this consequence as a life economy is assured provided sufficient kcal are available and can be acquired by activities in the style economy. One can live quite well either doing what one wants to do or nothing at all. I hold out Saudi Arabia as an example of the latter. The problem is that oil is a non-reproducible commodity and will one day run out while their population fails to learn the skills necessary for survival.

In a society where the population is stable and divided geographically the economy will stabilize as well. Market demand will be satisfied by workers accepting the lowest price for their labor, new entrants are discouraged from job hopping by the fact that market share cannot be achieved by lower prices only increased quality or output. In the case of sons and daughters wishing to replace their parents the children must share and they must accept whatever proportion the market affords them unless the market increases beyond the capability of the workforce to respond to it. It is assumed that even under ideal conditions those not normally considered as part of the normal workforce and or unemployed will step in to fill the gap. Such was the case when the United States entered World War II and tens of thousands of able workers were conscripted into the military. They were easily replaced by workers heretofore not in the workforce, namely women. That prices rose and labor costs skyrocketed was the result of not a shortage of labor but union pressure and unnecessary government interference such as price and wage control that thoroughly disrupted the normal reaction of a free economy. When it is not available you find substitutes and when there are no substitutes you do without. Since the market is limited to the distribution high value discretionary items can only be purchased through an accumulation of discretionary funds or loans that increase the cost but not the value of the purchase.

The spectrum of opportunities is constantly changing because we confuse societal growth with individual growth. An individual goes through the stages of growth, maturity, decline and death. This was indicated in Formula 1 by the term (i) that can be positive, zero or negative. A society goes through a stage of growth until its numbers reach that point where its reproducible natural resources can sustain the level of its population and reaches maturity. It can remain there only so long as this equality is maintained and will decline when it cannot. The style economy is cumulative but the life economy is not. The style economy will continue to grow so long as there are sufficient non-reproducible resources available and will begin to decline as they are used up and no replacements or substitutes can be found. It is accelerated by the growth in population which disguises the fact that world food production is not rising proportionately.

THE REAL ECONOMY

The obsession with societal growth is masked by the continual growth in population and the accelerated printing of paper money that has no backing save IOUs. Coupled with the fact that people must now work in order to survive, seek charity or obtain it from a government that has adopted a policy of wealth redistribution. Coincident with that is the continued loss of jobs because of government interference in the free market has priced labor out of the international market and an employer's first thought is can I recoup my labor cost at the world price for my output or must I make my product in another society if I am able. This instability is making it more difficult to determine which jobs and professions will be required.

Under the free market system of Republicanism the aforementioned situations cannot exist. So long as the economy is based on the kcal and the production of kcal from grains is sufficient to sustain the population Americans wishing or needing to work can earn a share of it in addition. That share however will be determined by the number of people competing and the number competing for the same job. The lifestyle made available by the distribution assure you can be whatever you want to be but whatever that is if you expect to do it to improve the lifestyle afforded you by nature you may have competition.

When a business gets beyond the individual entrepreneur and the partnership and begins hiring those who have no ownership stake in the firm the business assumes one of two characteristics. It is either project oriented or production oriented. A project oriented organization produces outputs that are finite in scope and time and demand is a significant variable and inestimable. A production oriented organization produces a known but continuous output until its market is sated or it creates a market that is itself continuous and sustaining. Neither of these is permanent and in order to survive and smooth out the swings in their respective markets the firms resort to subcontracting.in the case of project firms and outsourcing in the case of production firms.

The economy under Republicanism would not have seen the evolution of project oriented firms such as we see today because first of all the capital necessary to execute projects of the size seen today would not have been made available. Production firms would have evolved to produce today's products but much more slowly and not to such huge size. The reasons for this is that the banks are allowed to practice usury where they earn twice the loan amount if the interest rate is just over 3% per year for 30 years and considerably more as the interest rate rises. This is exacerbated by rising labor costs created by laws and regulations promulgated to allow labor to legally extort higher wages and benefits from their employer. These practices are encouraged by an unsuspecting public's enthusiasm for instant gratification and government's desire for control.

Just as the Pyramids and the great cathedrals of Europe were built over decades for the sole purpose of wealth distribution to assuage economically deprived citizens so too the U.S. government contrived the Hoover Dam, the TVA and CCC camps during the Great Depression. The current government subsidizes green energy and rail transportation projects and subsidizes other favored businesses, such as the defense industry, that will be a continual drag on the economy and with printed money no less. This would not have been necessary under Republicanism.

Value

Nature's bounty has no value until human intervention harvests it, mines it or manipulates it in such a way as to make it useful for consumption. If it is consumed, such as food, its value is lost. If it is retained its value will decrease at a rate proportional to the care exercised in its preservation and maintenance but will ultimately go to zero when it is either destroyed or deteriorates beyond repair. The value of anything can increase only if human effort enhances it.

Price

The price of anything is determined by what a buyer is willing to pay and a seller is willing to accept. Price equals value only at the point of the first sale. Subsequent sale of any item is subject to taxation only if no value is added. The tax shall be the difference in price between the selling price to the buyer and the purchase price to the seller and should the seller not be able to prove the price at the time of his purchase it shall be 100% of the selling price. In other words if there is no value added there is nothing gained. It is based on the premise that all things depreciate and reduce in value unless additional human effort is added. The rule is that since the N$ cannot appreciate in value, nothing purchased with it can either.

Theft

Emphasis has been placed on the concept of theft because it is the only individual right that needs to be prohibited in a society and to which government is established to prevent by defining what constitutes theft and to apprehend and punish those who do. Laws are a negative in that they prohibit certain actions. Regulations do not prohibit but regulate the exercise of human rights so as to protect individual health and safety and prevent infringement on the rights of others. The United States, having been established primarily by English Christians took their lead from the Ten Commandments that define the most common forms of theft including just thinking about it and the "Golden Rule" commonly understood to mean do unto others as you would have them do unto you. Unfortunately the implementation was left to the self-control of individuals and any punishment for wrongdoers was left in God's hands after death. Whether the framers of the U. S. Constitution believed the populous altruistic or purposefully left out punishment to protect the government that is now doing most of the stealing we will really never know for sure.

Socialism and communism promote sharing but fail to give recognition to the ability and contribution of the individual resulting in rewards to those unwilling to contribute. Monarchies and dictatorships, even benevolent ones enable a few to obtain a larger share of nature's bounty. Democracy is the worst of all because it lets the majority take the lion's share and is nearly impossible to overturn because the means of power is so close to the average and it takes so few to shift it from one to another and to hold on to.

Republicanism will never eliminate theft but with due diligence the people can assure their elected representatives are dissuaded from stealing from the people for they in essence will be stealing from themselves. It is assured by the fact nature's wealth is distributed to the people before the government gets their hands on it and the government only gets what the people are willing to give it. Only collusion between elected officials and the hired government present opportunities for theft when all wealth is distributed equally. It is patronage that enables the growth of government. It is assumed that the limited scope of government helped by the consequence of punishment will minimize these opportunities while maximizing the opportunity for oversight by the people.

Theft takes many forms and covetousness covers a lot of ground that needs a more appropriate explanation. For example, a company offers a two for the price of one or some other such temptation in order to win market share in hopes of being able to recoup the cost of the promotion and then put prices back up when the competition is forced out. This is using economic muscle to unfairly compete. This is theft and the punishment is that once the offer is made and product price reduced if it is raised, the excess profit is taxed away. It is not a punishment per se but a consequence if you attempt to gain market share with this tactic. If it is not, forfeiture of the license to do business will be.

Prevention

Prevention begins with making laws and regulations difficult to pass but easy to replace if they fail to achieve their objective. There are only so many kinds of theft and it has been easy to promulgate and apply laws to them. Regulations on the other hand place restrictions on people's natural rights and if containing outright prohibition constitute ex post facto laws and as such are prohibited. Regulation is just that, a means to regulate people's natural rights within limits proscribed by the society. As with criminal laws covering theft, both should require 90% of the vote to enact and only 51% to repeal if they are ineffective in achieving their objective.

If the punishment in being incarcerated or fined results in no violations it is not a reason to assume no laws or police are necessary because it only means the punishments meted out for violations get everyone to police their own actions. As we have seen, capital punishment has not deterred murder and wealthy people still steal. Speed limits are regulations as are all other measured regulations imposed to protect life and property. They are advisory and subject to conditions existing in particular cases. Germany has no speed limit on the Autobahns but you can be stopped by the police for what they consider driving to endanger; for example weaving in and out of traffic while doing 140 kilometers per hour. Even if the driver were a professional race car driver the others on the road are not. If in the opinion of the police you were driving to endanger results in an instantaneous fine of so many Deutschmarks for each km/hr. It is a very stiff fine and intended to encourage you to police yourself the next time and if you are caught again the fine goes up. The police are there to protect not only the public but you the offender and not for the sake of revenue. In the United States this has become a game firstly because the law is only meagerly enforced and in some cases deliberately not enforced on selected individuals and is open to bribery. The $20 bill handed over with the driver's license is only the tip of the iceberg and when the stakes are higher it is not uncommon for government officials to extort money from individuals who wish exception from the rules.

Theft is impossible to eliminate but the punishment can be raised to increase the risk beyond what the vast majority are willing to accept. In a society whose economic system is based on the kcal there is no need to steal to survive because the system guarantees it. Therefore, any theft has to be deliberate and intended to afford a better life style at another's expense. Based on the distribution incarceration and loss of it results in a benefit to society from the denial of most of it to cover only the cost of food, clothing and shelter. Deprivation and actual demonstrations of what happens to you when you steal serve as a further deterrent.

When the sentence is served the miscreant is returned to society with the proviso they can never qualify for employment in any government position or be elected to public office. Execution should be mandatory in cases of first degree murder unless a judge or jury sees fit to grant life as a ward of the state. Accidental death or manslaughter shall be mandatory incarceration or whatever restitution can be agreed with the surviving spouse, parent or guardian or closest relative an alternative available under Sharia Law.

A legislature's job in addition to making laws and regulations should be the proper enforcement of the law through oversight of the executive branch's enforcement practices and results. Like a board of directors it has oversight and control of the executive branch to the extent of approval and dismissal of its executives and the remuneration they receive for their services.

Government

With government severely restricted in its scope and nature's bounty distributed equally to all citizens it is unlikely that partisan politics would arise because no individual or group gains any advantage even at the state or local level. That all laws and regulations must be written so as to be applicable to everyone an incentive to politicize is mute. Still, a Constitution is predicated on the separation of powers so as to make any group in power unable to advantage themselves. The power in this case is to make or not enforce the law and the power of the purse through patronage.

One cannot begin to consider how to structure government without examining why all previous ones had failed. The framers of what became the U. S. Constitution failed in that attempt because they purposefully overlooked it. That is that government's only reason for existance is to prevent theft and since they came from governmental systems that allowed, if not encouraged theft and speculation with other people's money they were loath to create a system that not continue that tradition. In order to attain this they had to compromise with the smaller and poorer states in order to keep them in the fold and expand the number of victims they could exploit. A bicameral legislative body was totally unnecessary to achieve the sole objective of the Constitution and that was a mutual defense pact that would also create a uniform economic system for the thirteen states and any others that would be added. The fear of many of the framers that the federal government would ultimately make the states redundant was not unfounded.

The objective of a federal government is first to defend the states against foreign interests who would steal our lives, our freedom or our property. Second, it must establish a uniform system to allow the economy to work in such a way as to allow the States to protect the property of the people in a uniform way common to all the States. Very few federal laws are necessary to accomplish the first objective and the standards by which to achieve the second are already laid out in this paper and need only be adjusted if they fail to achieve their objective. Once established the focus of a national legislature shifts to one of audit to see that the executive branch and the judiciary perform their functions. The latter's as well as the Executive branch's sole responsibility is the carrying out of the law.

THE REAL ECONOMY

In constituting the legislature it is necessary to emphasize that each State is an equal to another. Funding of government is based on the distribution that takes the previous year's production of N$ and deducts the amount approved by the Congress to fund federal obligations and passes the remainder to the States on the basis of population. The States then deduct an amount approved by their legislature to fund their responsibilities and pass on an amount approved by the towns and cities to fund their people approved responsibilities. The remainder is then credited to each individual in kind with parents responsible for the accounts of their children until they become citizens. The State retains that portion that is allocated to wards of the State. The Town Treasurer, the State Treasurer and the Treasurer of the United States disburse the budgeted funds as necessary to the operating agencies. The books must balance for each at the end of the year and any surpluses added to the following year's distribution. No borrowing to cover shortfalls may be allowed.

If you examine the vast array of laws and regulations that have been enacted and imposed in a democracy, they fall into the category of either bills of attainder or ex post facto laws. As such, they are prohibited in a Republic. Without these, the number of laws and regulations can be severely reduced, meaning that legislators can spend the majority of their time overseeing the administration of those laws by the administrative branch of government. The administrative branch has no responsibility for creating the laws or regulations and its members are engaged as employees of the town, state and federal government and as such are engaged by the legislature and responsible to them for their performance. The legislature or a committee thereof acts as a board of directors. Legislator's performance is judged at the ballot box by the citizenry but legislators or administrative branch employees can be challenged by any citizen for breaking the law. If any such action is brought it takes precedence over any other activities being pursued by the courts.

The number of laws and regulations necessary in a Republic enables justice to be rendered by individuals not necessarily steeped in the law. The judiciary shall be a totally separate function and its members independently elected by the citizenry. Continuance in office shall be based on reaffirmation by 75% of the electorate each year unless removed for cause. Any citizen may challenge the conduct of any judge as regards commission of an actionable offense but not their judgment in specific cases except where the government itself is a party and the constitutionality of the law is in question. For example; a citizen questions the passage of a law exempting certain organizations or businesses they wish to encourage providing jobs for their unemployed. Under a Republican form of government such legislation is impossible because organizations or corporations are not regularly taxed again exposing the weaknesses of the current democratic form of government.

All power is vested in the citizen as regards the conduct of their representatives. To prevent abuse of this power challenges are taken seriously and if found valid a vindication of the veracity of Republicanism. However, with it comes the awesome responsibility of not being frivolous in what could mean the end of an individual's career or harm to their reputation. Significant fines should be imposed if an offense is alleged and later determined to be untrue.

Foreign Relations

George Washington, in his farewell address, cautioned against involvement in foreign intrigues. His advice has gone unheeded. How another society governs itself should be no business of another government. It is well to have relations with other societies no matter how they govern themselves because trade is the only means by which we can obtain things we do not make or the raw materials to make the things we do.

Free and open trade should always be the object recognizing that tariffs and subsidies are a mechanism employed by governments for economic and political reasons. In recognizing the legitimacy of another government should be on the basis of protecting one's citizens and the obligation of a government to be responsible for the actions of their citizens when in a country other than one's own. As such, the issuance of passports and visas is the mechanism employed to insure both the protection of one's citizens and to deny access to those likely to break the law. An American citizen convicted of a crime in the United States would be denied a passport and if already issued one it would have to be surrendered. If we had had an agreement with Saudi Arabia that provided we each are responsible for the acts of each other's citizens it is doubtful the terrorists who brought down the World Trade Center would have been issued a passport and the Saudis would have objected to our issuing them visas. In the event these safeguards were ineffective the Saudis would have been charged for the damages.

Defense

It is doubtful we would have ever reached the level of being able to annihilate just about everyone on earth if we had started out under Republican principles. As we are already there we can only benefit from the diversion of our resources to more positive pursuits with the caveat that we maintain a significant deterrent against attack. War is counterproductive unless you are prepared to overcome and annihilate your opposition. Winning a protracted war is next to impossible unless your opponent is in close proximity. In war there are no rules only victory or defeat. We have no business and no authority to be fighting a war on another country's territory unless that country first attacked us. We certainly have no business in being mercenaries to governments fighting their own people in order to retain power. At this point in the history of civilization a war against another country, even those who are barely able to defend themselves would incur losses far in excess of anything that might be gained. Those countries that do have something to gain are proof of the previous statement. Only the Soviet Union and the United States currently have fighting troops on the ground in countries other than their own and are fighting as mercenaries not to defend the lives, liberties and property of their own people but those of the government they are supporting.

Crime and Punishment

No system is perfect but, a minimalist system is the easiest to control and keep within acceptable limits. Republicanism is designed to distribute nature's wealth evenly at a minimum and any extra as a consequence of application of human capital whose acquisition is available to those who wish to acquire it. Still there will be those who want more and are unwilling to make the effort to obtain it legitimately. The law is intended to punish those who do and knowledge of that punishment serve as a deterrent to others.

The Republican economic system provides a minimum standard of living wherein the only necessity to steal comes when there is insufficient kcal to feed the entire population. Until that time theft of any kind is voluntary and premeditated. The distribution provides a means for the restoration of monetary loss to the victims of most theft but it is not sufficient to punish the act. Denial of the opportunity to improve one's style of life for a period is the most humane way of punishing those who are dissatisfied with their lot, does not burden society and does not deny others the opportunity to do so. There is something drastically amiss in a society when a lawbreaker is treated better than a law abiding citizen. Individuals or organizations who believe this punishment unfair cannot be prohibited from supplementing the miscreant's distribution but it must be pure charity without strings and not in compensation for services that the benefactor would have to procure from law abiding citizens. In addition the individual or the organization would have to name themselves or someone in the organization who would be an accomplice should the miscreant repeat his offense or any other.

Banking and Credit

Theft cannot be imaginary. When it occurs there is evidence that it has been committed and a person or persons committed it. When not caught in the act it is more difficult to prove guilt than it is innocence. Under Republicanism the accumulation of wealth is not a crime but a mark of prudence and achievement. Earned wealth is easily explained and evidenced. Unearned wealth will therefore show up in the accumulation of unearned credit in one's bank account or the sequestration of unearned currency. The banking system under Republicanism can be equipped with built in triggers to detect unusual transactions that could be challenged for their legality. It is built on the premise that an individual or corporate entity can have but one account and all of the banks are connected to prevent the opening of multiple accounts by a single entity.

Under a Republican economy currency or credits can leave the country in the process of trade. The exchange of currency or credits can only be legitimately conducted through the nation's central banks. When a transaction is made the importing country's bank converts the importer's currency into the exporting country's currency charging a fee for the transaction. If the importer's bank does not have the currency of the transaction it must buy it on the currency market. This method of exchange does not create more currency for international trade and the actual currency obtained by the exporting country has no value until redeemed to affect another transaction. All currencies are not equal. Most are because they are measured by their reserves in dollars as opposed to gold. Currencies that are not linked to the US $ and not traded on the currency markets are those whose import and export are strictly prohibited to protect their internal purchasing power. How and to whom that currency is distributed makes no difference to the value of the transaction, its value in whatever currency does. The Republican economy is based on the life economy. Therefore the kcal has the same value everywhere and the local currency has that value no more or less. The value of these accounts in foreign currency compared to the N$

then needs to be determined.

As I have used the base year of 1914 for the determination of the value of N$ it is appropriate to use the exchange rates in use at that time as a starting point. The problem arises that the economy of all countries is now driven by the style economy rather than the life economy and even countries that have surplus kcal to sell are now required to subsidize agricultural producers in order to produce them. The rates, though valid for the current world are invalid as regards the currency manipulations and economic practices not associated with a Republican free market economy.

The first step in the process of determining a proper exchange rate is to take the current rate equated to the US$ then take out the manipulation of the US$ to arrive at the N$ equivalent exchange. For example, the Euro trades at $1 = €0.80 but it takes $13.01 to buy what $1 did in 1914 in terms of kcal. Therefore in N$ the Euro is equivalent to N$.061 and so on for all the other major currencies except for China.

Chinese currency is not traded on the world market. The Chinese economy of today is less than 75 years old and up until recently did not engage in capitalist practices. Its basis, like that of the U.S. dollar is the full faith and credit of the government of China. The difference being China has to import food whereas the U. S. has a large surplus. The Chinese economy exploded when opportunities to exploit its cheap labor were opened with the U. S. tariff removals occasioned by trade agreements that were decidedly one sided. When it did, it produced surpluses that could be sold for dollars. The Yuan, as evidenced by the fact they had to import kcal any introduction of excess currency would result in inflation. In order to prevent this from happening the Chinese Central Bank only introduced as much new currency as was spent in producing the export surplus. The remainder was used to procure the kcal on the world market. It could therefore use what remained to purchase the bonds of whatever country it chose. Smartly it chose the U.

S. knowing it would be the last country to default on its loans because of our agricultural surplus. This is how the British arbitraged gold until that practice was taken over by the Americans. They will be able to arbitrage the U. S. dollar in this fashion until the U. S. starts consuming all the kcal it produces internally.

Paper money is not yet obsolete and is still the most convenient and necessary for personal transactions. People are not yet ready to carry around wireless card readers although they are now readily available. The drawback of course is when the battery is dead or the electricity fails commerce stops. Policing when large transfers of cash are deposited to individual accounts is relatively easy and can be well monitored. At the end of each year all surplus currency would be turned in to the bank and individual accounts credited and the currency destroyed. This would prevent the development of an underground cash economy. In other words, the present currency will no longer be valid after a specified date and the following years currency issues would be completely different. It would not only help reveal unusual accumulations but also discourage counterfeiters and money theft.

Taxation

With a government funded through budgets and the distribution, taxation as we know it is unnecessary except to thwart monopoly practices by individuals or enterprises. There are however ventures that are beneficial to a society as a whole that are best addressed by a government of the people. I refer to public utilities such as water supply, garbage and sewage disposal, electricity and public transportation. These are common needs or benefits made possible either by nature or the common needs or wants by all. If left to private development, only those that provided a profit on the service would be served but in order to provide it the private enterprise would have to make use of land or other assets that belong to the public. The solution to these opportunities or needs is the public utility or corporation. In essence a government established monopoly. It should be remembered that when societies were small all of these services were made possible by private enterprise and it is only the increase in population that has made it necessary for the public to intervene through government in order that all the people be served, not just those for whom it is profitable.

The reason private enterprise does not voluntarily enter into these areas is their high capital cost. Private enterprise cannot raise the necessary capital to serve the entire population if it cannot recover its investment in the form of fees. This is already being accomplished by private enterprise who can obtain bank financing when they are offered a return on their investment by a borrower who is given a monopoly by the government. The problems arise when the service provider must then obtain approval of government regulators to raise fees or rates to cover their additional costs due to government interference in the free market, primarily with actions such as the imposition of minimum wages. The end result is few are willing to enter such arrangements and in the end fewer people are served and the service becomes undependable. I cite the U. S. Post Office and Amtrak as classic cases where instead of abandoning these services when private enterprise was able to siphon customers by cheaper and more efficient service they desperately hang on to them to protect jobs and votes. These however are dwarfed by the military industrial complex whose job it is to supply the forces deemed necessary to defend the country.

The defense component of the economy now comprises over 25% of the federal budget much of it spent not defending the United States but fighting wars and defending other countries.

This spending is justified by a position that the military be ready to fight a land war on both coasts simultaneously. Such a position is indefensible on its face when an enemy would have to cross two oceans with sufficient men, equipment and supplies and be undetected until it landed. It would have to carry with it sufficient food until it reached the Midwestern States since that is where the bulk of the surplus exists. In order to make such an effort the invading party would have to accept huge losses and in order to achieve any gain would have to eliminate all occupants, the initial objective being to obtain sufficient land to feed a starving domestic population who would then have to occupy the country in order to grow sufficient food to feed them. While the world watches this is exactly what is occurring in Africa and the Middle East. It is even occurring in Israel where the Jewish population is trying to recover land they lost long ago. To be successful they must takeover sufficient land to feed the population and since it is already limited their survival depends on help from the outside while they force out the Palestinians who are fighting to get their land back.

Under the current system, projects such a cooperative effort to harness our rivers, generate electric power, conserve and divert water to where it is needed are never undertaken but those to put a man on the moon are. It is an insane disorder of priorities but our government looks only to what can satisfy today and ignores what will be tomorrow.

The Future

The future of America is illustrated by the wheat production per person as illustrated in Figure 1. Agricultural technology has increased the yield per acre to where we now average 45 bushels per acre and we may have already reached the limit where the ability to push this higher is questionable. Complaints are already being made that this increase is due primarily to genetically modified seed whose long term deleterious effects have yet to be uncovered if they exist at all. In addition we are actually reducing the number of acres being planted. Farmers are already switching to more profitable crops and along with other countries the United States has been subsidizing grain producers for some years to meet world demand. The same is true for rice, particularly in Asia. We actually buy wheat from Canada because it can produce it for less than the subsidized U. S. price. Another sign of the impending collapse is the fact we import enough kcal in the form of high labor cost food to feed over 8 million people while at the same time exporting our surplus grains. The only reason many Americans survive is that the government is providing the funds through programs such as SNAP.

Based on the trend rather obvious in the period between 1985 and 2014 the number of bushels per person will be down to 1 in about 2064. This presumes no change in yield or acreage and population growth at current levels. Unlike the predictions of Thomas Malthus there will not be any precipitous crash in the economy but a steady decline as foodstuffs now used for other purposes and the feeding of animals is shifted to human consumption. The latter assumes, unlike the majority who enjoyed a surplus during the Irish Potato Famine, are willing to share that surplus. Mexico the source of the majority of our food imports will or already has become like Israel and maxed out in the amount of its low kcal food production and will be unable to supply the increasing U.S. demand further inflating prices and will be hurt by the unavailability of U. S. surpluses. The situation will be exacerbated by the influx of even greater numbers of refugees primarily from Latin America because of the ease of entry.

Figure 1 - U. S. Wheat Harvest

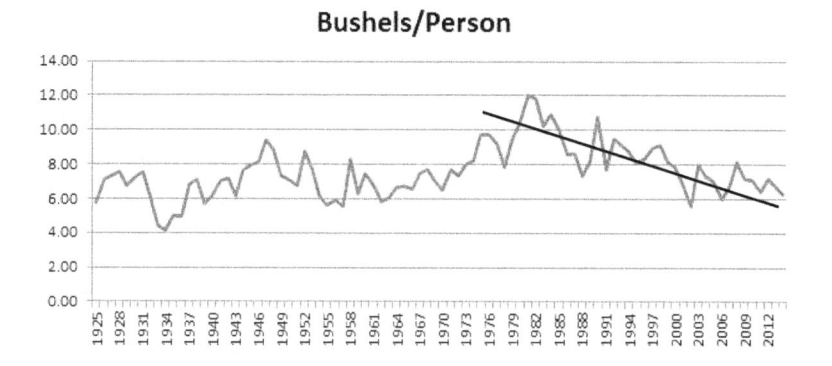

Bushels/Person

The Real Threat to an American Utopia

Based on the United Nations Food and Agriculture Organization statistics for 2012 Latin America has a kcal factor of 1.52, dangerously close to subsistence and hence sensitive to variations in climate and water supply. It has already reached a level where near to starving people are migrating north. Mexico is already down to 0.9 and fighting between the people and the cartels that actually run the country has already begun. Only Ecuador, Uruguay, Guyana, Paraguay and Argentina are above the average.

We are not the only ones suffering the influx of migrants. England has seen the influx of Indians and Pakistanis, Commonwealth members when the British Empire flourished who not only emigrated to England but other Commonwealth countries and Africa. Australia is bearing the influx of immigrants from Asia and Europe is seeing them from Africa and the Middle East. Land bridges make it nearly impossible to stop or even to police. The problem is created by government control of the food distribution system exacerbated by the lack of population control.

The vicious cycle has already begun where government induced inflation requires an even greater printing of money creating higher inflation in a never ending chase for survival.

Currently Europe is seeing an increasing influx of immigrants and refugees from Africa and the Middle East. Greece and the other Mediterranean countries do not have the agricultural surpluses to support them so they are migrating to France, the UK and Scandinavia not all of whom want them. It is a continuing influx that has no end because these people are escaping virtual starvation imposed on them by regimes that control the distribution of the very food needed to sustain life through employment.

Epilogue

It is not impossible to wipe the slate clean and start over. A change to Republicanism would of course be sweeping to the two ends of the income spectrum with those who have benefited most from the unfair system of democracy having their largess reined in. They could still keep what they have accumulated but see its real value severely reduced. At the other end, there would be no poor and even those unable to participate could lead a full life. They are few in number and much that would come to them in the distribution they are currently obtaining through government welfare schemes.

What is transpiring in Africa and the Middle East and is starting in Mexico is the metastasizing of the cancer that is population growth; Malthus saw it and his predictions were ignored. Even if we should become one world without borders and a single Republican government, without population control we will ultimately be fighting each other over food and it is probably only decades away at the most. Japan is seeing a natural decline in its population and has virtually no immigration. Perhaps it is because its life factor is less than 0.7 and it must import a substantial amount of its food. It is in better shape than China to thwart migration, being an island country.

'We are already at war with Mexico and fail to realize it. Millions of Mexicans have invaded us without benefit of a Trojan horse because, for the most part, we conveniently look the other way or actually invite them to do the manual labor tasks our own population will not do because to do so would reduce their welfare or unemployment payments. Our government, Republicans and Democrats fight to keep them here in order to obtain or retain their vote to stay in power. The actual number is unknown because our governmental system is incapable of actually counting them. The same is true for the legal population and the total error might be close to 10% of the known population. The loyalty of these illegal aliens becomes quite evident when they feel their privileges are threatened. The Mexican flags come out in force.

THE REAL ECONOMY

Why are they coming here? Whether they trek from South or Central America and can run the gauntlet of oppression from the Mexican drug cartels who actual run Mexico or are Mexicans themselves they are fleeing oppression and actual starvation because if they cannot work they cannot eat. In my lifetime I have seen the population of the United States nearly triple. I doubt the government even knows how many people there really are and the estimates of illegals ranges from 12-20 million and they are the biggest contributors to the population growth. More disturbing in the Border States is the fact that English speaking whites and even Asians are being displaced by Spanish speaking Latinos and the homes in which they live are increasingly Spanish speaking. Government catering to non-English speakers is increasingly evident in the fact the naturalization exam questions can now be obtained in Spanish as well as other languages. Most disturbing of course is the fact that this is no longer a possibility but an ever increasingly predictable outcome. Every parent says they want to leave something better for their children. Up until the 1980s this may have been the case but, in the United States this is no longer possible.

Under our current political system it would take an epiphany by a majority of our elected leaders to stop the slide and to do so would require a complete abandonment of the old economic system. The old economic systems were salvaged because the medium of exchange could be devalued and the production of the real medium of exchange outpacing its consumption. The world is now consuming its surpluses and in some countries they are no longer able to feed the growing population. That problem is soon to be with us and we cannot devalue the kcal to solve it. To top it off we have a government bureaucracy that has resorted to hiding the facts and their trends in order to justify itself and claim all is well. They claim unemployment figures without the real ability to actually count those who are working, let alone unemployed. They give us population figures based on sampling and not actual head counting and yet tell us how many unemployed there are in the country when there is no possible way to count them.

THE REAL ECONOMY

Most destructive are the estimates of future deficits when they know for certain that future expenditures by government will rise and deficits will continue to grow because all the factors that influence these trends are moving in a negative direction. These deficits decrease the purchasing power of the dollars being printed to stem the gap and are permanent and irreversible.

We are already like Greece but have no Germany to rescue us from ourselves and no will to reduce our lifestyle to accommodate reality.

7

INFLATION

There are two types of monetary disturbances; currency inflation and cost inflation. Currency inflation occurs when the amount of money in circulation increases and the value decreases. The situation in Germany after World War I will serve to illustrate this. Cost inflation occurs when prices increase without commensurate increase in value.

The peace treaty signed after the war required Germany to make payments to the victors in the international trading unit which was ounces of gold. The German Mark was backed by gold and to simplify the calculations let us assume the German Central Bank had 100 billion ounces of gold and had issued 100 billion Marks making 1 Mark equal to 1 ounce of gold. If the payment was say 10 billion ounces the Central Bank sent 10 million ounces of gold to the victors. Instead of calling in 10 billion Marks in taxes or borrowing 10 billion Marks against future taxes it merely printed 10 billion in additional Mark notes. The situation this created is there are now 110 million Marks outstanding but only 90 million ounces of gold in support making the Mark equal to 0.82 ounces of gold on the world market or a dilution in the value of the Mark. If the next payment was equal to the first the resultant is the same but the numbers are now increasing exponentially because the actual weight of the gold is decreasing. The concept is similar to compound interest but instead of increasing in value the value is decreasing. It is similar to the half-life of elements that give off radiation in the process of decay. Germany finally put a stop to inflation by revaluing the Mark and stopping the reparations payments.

INFLATION

Countries like Brazil and Argentina have come upon this scenario more slowly as the amount of gold being produced kept declining as its sources petered out. Effects of currency inflation began when the deficiency in the amount of locally produced gold could not be offset with gold obtained through exports and borrowing as opposed to taxation became necessary to balance the economy. Several devaluations and government changes occurred until the United States, after the end of World of World War II convened a world monetary conference in Breton Woods, New Hampshire where the world's bankers agreed to peg the value of gold at $35 per ounce. The market value of gold in 1914 was about $18 an ounce but was beginning to rise commensurate with its cost of production. This finally put the lie to the fact that gold, or any other commodity other than the kcal itself could serve as a proxy for use in measuring the economy. The façade was finally lifted in 1973 when the United States no longer recognized the gold standard allowing the dollar to float; prior to that the U. S. Treasury no longer offered to exchange dollars for gold.

Cost inflation is the consequence of the rise in cost of subsequent units of production. This can occur because of a rise in cost of raw materials or the rise in wages as a result of an uncompetitive labor market. Gold is the classic case in that the cost of its production has risen due to the increase in the amount of labor required to convert the impure raw material to obtain a pure product. If labor is also able through collective bargaining to increase its compensation without a commensurate increase in production the unit cost of their output increases. This is only possible if the employer is unable or prohibited from replacing them with workers who will perform the same task for less which is exactly the situation under the NLRB Act.

8
THE FUEL CONSUMPTION EQUATION

It has been demonstrated that man requires about 2500 kcal per day of fuel to be active about half that time making him about 50% efficient as an engine. To survive he must then obtain or be given 2500 kcal per day in fuel. The following formula demonstrates first that it takes at least two people for both to survive if one does nothing to obtain sufficient kcal on his own. Second, if one can obtain sufficient kcal for both, the time necessary to obtain it for one must be half or less than that for one.

If T is working time and t is idle time the following equation applies:

$$T + t = 24 \text{ hours}$$

If fuel burning is considered T must be the residual of 24 - t and vice versa

$$\text{Then } T \times aF + t \times bF = 2500 \text{ kcal}/24$$

Where F is the amount of fuel burned per hour and a and b are variables ranging between 0 and 24

It has been postulated that either T or t must be ≤ 24 and the only way they can be equal is if they are both 12. We have also said that T cannot be more than 12 on a continuous basis so it would mean obtaining

THE FUEL CONSUMPTION EQUATION

twice the fuel consumed meaning if b = 0 a must be 2 but it cannot because it would require burning twice as many kcal as obtained. The human body is designed to be about 50% efficient and produce a sustained output of 0.1 horsepower. It is capable of sporadic outputs of considerably more but these are not sustainable and additional kcals are required to produce them because they involve muscular effort.

One human can survive if provided 2500 kcal per day but if they cannot perform the functions necessary to obtain them will ultimately die. Therefore in order to survive those who cannot must have someone who will obtain them when t = 24. This is possible on condition that everyone is given the wherewithal to purchase the time of others when they cannot fend for themselves and there is someone with the time to sell.

9
THE DEMISE OF THE DINOSAURS

Creatures of the Jurassic period, the dinosaurs, were carnivorous or herbivorous. They lived in balance so long as there was enough for them to eat. That balance was determined by nature insuring that their numbers could grow to a point only to that where each had sufficient food to eat. That is the earth produced enough food for the herbivores and enough herbivores for the carnivores. The number of herbivores was limited to half the number that could be supported by the area they grazed leaving sufficient uneaten food in order to propagate and replace that which was eaten while they moved to the other half the grazing area to repeat the process.

The carnivore's upper limit was determined by twice the number of herbivores before they would have to start eating each other in order to survive. The control and balance of this entire scenario is dependent on the food available to the herbivores because their numbers are dependent on the amount of food they have to eat. If the food supply is too much for their number, their number can increase or it goes to waste until the number of herbivores increases, allowing that of the carnivores to increase. In this new scenario it is still required that the herbivores continue to leave behind in the forage area sufficient seed in order to reproduce itself.

Given no other event such as disease, lack of rain or some other outside

THE DEMISE OF THE DINOSAURS

predator on their ecosystem, this cycle still has a limit and that is the depletion of the solid nutrients necessary for the growth of forage plants and water. Over time these nutrients are depleted and the crop size steadily deteriorates unless they are made up by new ones brought in by the wind or the rain. This may take a considerable time, not the short time supposedly indicated by the rapid demise of the dinosaurs.

It is my theory that the herbivores began starving to death because of a rapid reduction in their food supply created by the saturation of their numbers. Let's assume that the number of herbivores increased by one from saturation where there was enough to eat for the previous number and they were insured enough to eat the next time if they accidentally left 10 % of it behind to reproduce, rot or be consumed by smaller animals, birds or insects. It would not immediately allow for an increase in the carnivore population because they could not be in a one to one ratio or there would be no herbivores and hence no carnivores. It is a similar analogy with elands and lions today in Africa. The extra herbivore has to consume some of the food normally being left behind reducing the amount available to propagate the next crop. This reduces the crop for the next cycle and since the herbivores do not cultivate the soil they can never make up the difference and they eat it all in one cycle and there is none at all and the herbivores disappear. In the meantime the carnivores, running out of herbivores begin eating themselves meaning of course they start with the young who cannot defend themselves and so on until the last one starves to death. Whether it is male or female is totally academic. Once the depletion starts it can be slowed or accelerated by external factors but not stopped.

10

RESTORING THE AMERICAN DREAM

It took less than two centuries for Americans to cast off the yoke of British rule and to forge a new path to freedom under a road map never before conceived. It took less than two years for the country's leadership to stray and begin a new journey which has seen many fits and starts. In less than a century the southern agricultural states tried to take a different path but were forced to return in a war whose after-effects are still being felt. Some would have you believe the Civil War was fought over slavery because they wish to deny the fact that it was really a state's rights issue. They want you to believe them because if it was the latter reason they would also have to admit they denied the southern states what they claimed was the right of all free people in the Declaration of Independence. "That when any form of government becomes destructive of these ends, it is the right of the people to alter or to abolish it, and to institute new government".

Each time we came to a fork in the road we chose to compromise and take the middle. Unlike the Jews who wandered in the wilderness for forty years before finding the Promised Land we have now been wandering for over two hundred and find ourselves still hopelessly lost and fraught with problems that, like the Gordian knot, defy solution. This chapter posits what we could have done to avoid our present dilemma and its probable causes and considers it is not too late to turn back to the map we started with and continue the journey under a free market economy that will return the freedom we have lost and restore the American dream we envisioned.

The American Dream

The American dream is possible because nature supplies the necessities of life and obtaining them has required less and less time and effort such that the time saved can be put to improving the style of life. Instead of distributing nature's wealth equally among its citizens, all systems of government devised to date have placed themselves in a position at the top of the food chain enabling them to allocate that wealth unevenly to themselves and the supporters who have given them that power. Under the U. S. Constitution the Congress's greatest power is not to tax but to coin money, regulate the value thereof and of foreign coin, a power that has been woefully abused. When politicians found they could abuse this power without punishment it signaled the end of the journey as the framers may have envisioned it. The only thing that can save it is a return to a free market economy regulated by the Republican model where government's sole role is to distribute nature's bounty equally among all its citizens and to seek out and punish those who would steal it from them including the government itself. It can be done, indeed it must be done, and the only ones whose bounty would be diminished are those who benefitted from past abuses.

Genesis

No sooner was the ink dry on the Constitution Alexander Hamilton the Treasury Secretary of the United States had his supporters in the Congress pass a law creating a national bank. George Washington was at first reluctant to sign it and commissioned his Attorney General Edmund Randolph and his Secretary of State Thomas Jefferson and Hamilton to give him a written opinion as to the Constitutionality of the law. The foundation of Hamilton's argument rests on two principles and was stated in the very first part of his brief:

1. In entering upon the argument, it ought to be premised that the objections of the Secretary of State and Attorney General are founded on a general denial of the authority of the United States to erect corporations. The latter, indeed, expressly admits that if there be anything in the bill which is not warranted by the Constitution, it is the clause of incorporation.

2. Now it appears to the Secretary of the Treasury that this general principle is inherent in the very definition of government, and essential to every step of progress to be made by that of the United States, namely: That every power vested in a government is in its nature sovereign, and includes, by force of the term, a right to employ all the means requisite and fairly applicable to the attainment of the ends of such power, and which are not precluded by restrictions and exceptions specified in the Constitution, or not immoral, or not contrary to the essential ends of political society.

The validity of the first argument is predicated on the validity of the second. The United States of America as covered by the Constitution is not a sovereign state but a mutual defense pact with limited and specified powers and an association of sovereign states. The second argument is one of the end justifies the means an argument that would be made again in 1819 in McCulloch versus Maryland (17 US 316) and thence codified into law by Justice John Marshall a judgment that would make the United States of America a sovereign government and the states redundant. In that judgment Marshall opined, "If the end be legitimate and within the scope of the Constitution, all the means which are appropriate, which are plainly adapted to that end, and which are not prohibited, may constitutionally be employed to carry it into effect." With that decision the United States ceased to be a Republic and became a democracy with a government of nearly limitless power. Democracy is the most heinous of governments in that it is hard to replace and a simple majority may force its will on the minority and deprive it of all of its rights.

Neither Jefferson nor Randolph objected to banks per se but believed its functions could be best carried out by the states. Their constitutional argument was based on the limited powers given the federal government none of which could be stretched to include the chartering of corporations and the establishment of a bank. Needless to say they not only lost the argument but ultimately the principal with Marshall's edict.

The banking system in the United Sates was a mirror image of that of Great Britain. Instead of just a repository for the safe keeping of assets its profits rested on its ability to collect usury and to create money. Both these functions run afoul of the basic tenet of a free society in that "Thou Shalt Not Steal". The first is making money on money and was the reason for Christ throwing the money-changers out of the temple. In a free economy one may charge for the services necessary to arrange and collect a loan but not an interest that would collect more than what was borrowed. The latter is plain fraud. It should be noted that under Muslim Sharia law charging or paying interest is forbidden.

11

POWER TO THE PEOPLE

Power is money and money is power. Therefore they are equals. Like the chicken and the egg, which came first? The only answer is that they arrived simultaneously. The ones who have it or have just acquired it loathe giving it up and it must be wrested away by force and once acquired the cycle begins again.

Since his banishment from the Garden man has sought to be one with nature. As soon as he succeeded he was confronted by another who had failed and if lucky could placate his adversary by sharing his surplus. If not, his adversary, if he could, took his place at being one with nature. The inability to temper reproduction habits meant constant pressure on the food supply and migration was becoming a problem because most places they could go were now populated by people who didn't want them so the land had to be taken by force, the leaders promising spoils to the troops (peasants) and land to the officers (tribal leaders) hence ownership of the food supply and the power of distribution.

These types of wars have never ceased but have diminished in size because the wealthy countries are strong enough to make trade and accommodation a less costly endeavor. In the process of ever increasing population the style economy has dwarfed the life economy and the manhours devoted to agriculture are but a fraction of those devoted to other activities. As a result, maintenance of the life economy has been short changed in the allocation of land and governments must now subsidize the basic food commodities in order to retain adequate supply. In the process of this evolution, leadership and the allocation of nature's wealth has shifted from the land owners to the industrialists and hence from a long range maintenance philosophy to a short term opportunity philosophy.

The unabated growth of population has resulted in problems of crisis proportions because the world, ruled and managed by short term thinkers, has failed to recognize the limits of agriculture which maintains and drives both economies. As a consequence governments have resorted to all sorts of contrivances to retain power, the last resort being borrowing not realizing this only prolongs the inevitable and risks the chance that when the government leadership falls new leadership could shift back to the people instead of the entrenched bureaucracy. The lenders are complicit in this action to retain the bureaucracy because they too will inherit this same dilemma if the borrower's tumult results in civil war and the creation of more refugees fleeing to the lenders country triggering a repeat of the same cycle.

Greece is the classic case and an omen of things to come and a lesson that history has not learned and therefore repeated. Its wealth has been squandered on the large government apparatus that has built up over the decades. Now beholden to the moneyed countries of the Eurozone for their survival the government reluctantly agrees to reforms it knows it will not be able to impose for fear it will be thrown from power. When it tries the great government bureaucracy that includes the government pensioners and others dependent on government largess riots, ousts the government and the lenders rush in to repeat the process. The ousted accept their lot or migrate. When and if they do they are quickly replaced by even more from Africa and the Middle East whose problems are even more severe. The only comparison to this is the metastasizing of cancer in the human body which if not removed in its infancy will soon spread beyond control.

The bureaucracy is like the Hydra of Greek mythology. When one head was cut off it grew two more in its place. According to legend Heracles' nephew assisted in the task of slaying the Hydra by cauterizing the neck of the severed head so it would not grow back until Heracles finally severed the immortal head. The lesson is that once a bureaucracy forms you may cut off its head and another will arise to take its place so you must slay all of them if there is to be change. The framers of the U. S. Constitution made this difficult, if not impossible, at the ballot box because only 1/3 of the Senate is changed in each voting cycle. It is an error repeated in most of the States and municipalities. It was not lost on the Democrats as they have done everything possible to dissuade anyone from taking leadership of the Tea Party and harnessing and focusing its energy.

Revolts by those getting the short end of a diminishing stock are becoming more common and their inevitability is preceded by migration. We are being given a glimpse of the inevitable and those having the power to alter the course of history by prolonging it for our progeny are afraid to take the actions necessary because they will lose the power they covet. When the light seemed to be at the end of a very long tunnel there was no need or desire for the drastic action necessary. The tunnel has not gotten shorter it is just that for centuries we have been going in the wrong direction, back into the darkness and it is time to change direction before what appears to be a light at the end goes out. My calculations indicate that unless we do, the point of no return will be reached before the end of this century.

12

IMPLEMENTING THE IMPOSSIBLE

This chapter will be divided into two parts. The first part will discuss implementation of a Republican form of government that may be installed through the ballot box. The second will discuss how it may be accomplished through peaceful revolution. It can always be accomplished with a successful armed revolt providing there are enough adherents to overcome the expected armed opposition.

The Legitimate Approach

The Republican Party must be convinced that their objective of minimalist government can only be achieved if they agree that it will ultimately be put out of the currency distribution business. The corollary of course is it will also put the Democrat Party out of business as well and we will eliminate what George Washington cautioned against in the beginning and that was partisan politics.

We are at a critical crossroads where the House of Representatives is in the hands of the Republicans and Republicans can thwart any Democrat Legislation in the House and we have the Democrat President ruling by selective application of the law and Executive Orders. The Supreme Court has been mostly neutralized wanting to appease the Democrats by not declaring laws previously passed by them as unconstitutional or not getting cases by the Executive's Justice Dept. deliberately dragging cases through myriad courts or pushing them to the bottom of the pile so they don't even get a hearing. This fortuitous opportunity should not be wasted.

Some one of the numerous candidates now vying for an opportunity to be President should try and convince them that if restoring America is their mutual objective they will only be able to do so if they cease competing with each other, focus on a single objective and do their utmost to elect more Republicans of like mind and are willing to sacrifice the party for the common good. They must be convinced to be altruistic and that what they are doing is likely to put them out of a job. Then they must choose two of their number or even ones outside that group whom they believe stand the best chance of winning a general election. It would be well if they were then each assigned a so-called shadow cabinet post to be able to explain to the voters how they would dismantle the behemoth that is destroying the country, usurping the people's freedom and stealing their property.

The biggest obstacle in implementing the foregoing is internal. There are too many Republicans who like their counterparts in the Democrat Party that are obsessed with power and although tout small government are really saying "I'm for small government so long as I control it". As long as this thought dominates the party they can continue to flaunt the Constitution which at this point is little more than an historic document since its limitations and requirements no longer halt or even inhibit those in power. As stated in a previous chapter you cannot have your cake and eat it too is false until you run out of flour. Unfortunately the rot has metastasized and the chances of the above occurring are worse than one hundred to one.

Internal Revolt

The Declaration of Independence gives license to an internal revolt by stipulating when a government is destructive of the peoples' lives, their liberties and their pursuit of happiness they have a right to alter or abolish it. The problem comes in exercising that right.

The revolutionary patriots who defeated the British Army were opposing a formidable foe. They were fortunate in the fact that their opposition had a long yet vulnerable supply line and no clear objective to fight for save obeying their masters who were 3000 miles away They were also better armed but the replenishment of ammunition for those arms was vulnerable and at the end of a 3000 mile supply line. It was not trained in guerilla tactics by a well-armed militia force that had the support or at least the acquiescence of the populous. Thankfully, despite a nearly continuous need of supplies that were doggedly proffered due to lack of funds and some serious ineptitude in tactics, the revolutionaries prevailed and the English surrendered.

Whatever tactics are to be employed they must be swift, deliberate and focused. A military response by the entrenched power must either be subverted to support the revolt or neutralized to stand back. Key officials who can summon resistance must be immediately neutralized. The coup group must be small, dedicated and operate under the guise of a mass rally that is totally unaware they are part of the plot until it is being carried out. Mass public support for the action can only be assured if the coup group leader has wide support among the massed public and that his intentions are honorable, without it the coup will fail.

History demonstrates that few coups have been successful and those that have merely resulted in replacing corrupt officials with those that will soon be corrupted. Egypt, Libya, Somalia, Syria, Iraq and Afghanistan are the most recent examples. Ancient Greece and the Roman Empire fared no better. Present day Greece is about to go down and will soon be followed by Italy, Spain and Portugal. In over 5000 years of recorded history no one has yet gotten it right.

13

THE FINAL ARBITRAGE

We are already entering the final phase of the economic cycle that consists of four basic elements. These are discovery, growth, maturity and decline. The Mayans are gone, the Incas are gone, the Aztecs are gone as are the Pharaohs, the Greek and Roman Empires and the Dynasties of Japan and China. The British Empire is no more and the American Empire really never was, but big enough to make a mark on history. The Chinese are making a vain attempt at slowing it but have succumbed to the pressures of greed like those before them. It started with food and will end with food or rather the lack of it. In over ten thousand years of recorded history man has yet to learn that despite his best efforts natures' resources are finite and even those which can be reproduced and multiplied will ultimately be depleted because they too need non-reproducible commodities such as water in order to reproduce. That some want more than their share just speeds the depletion. It is no honor to have borne witness to the time when the decline started.

The Food and Agriculture Organization (FAO) of the United Nations has been sounding the alarm about the growing world agricultural deficiency. It has gone unnoticed in most places and insufficiently in all because the U. N. and all of its member countries have failed to recognize their measurements have all been based on false proxies represented by metals and paper exchange. Because of this two economies have been created as described in this paper. They are inextricably linked because the life economy, although now much smaller in measure than the other they must be equal. One can only consume what one produces.

THE FINAL ARBITRAGE

It is uncertain as to when societies shifted from being custodians and sharers of nature's wealth to ownership but it meant the basis of who got the lion's share of that wealth no longer depended on the value of individual contribution to the common weal. There should be no doubt that it was the consequence of societies forced to stealing in order to survive and when dividing up the spoils, the society's leaders got the land.

Natural and artificial borders have compartmentalized or comingled societies and those who possess the wealth continue to accumulate the bulk of the ever dwindling nonrenewable natural resources while ignoring the shift their excess has enabled to less efficient renewable resources. The latter deprives the poorest segment of access to the least expensive foods for even survival. If one must now work for a living or accept charity for survival one must resort to theft if neither is available. Individually one can opt to migrate to where work or charity is available or as the numbers of destitute increase try to switch places with the established hierarchy through organized theft. Collective theft from a neighboring society is unlikely to be successful because the price of victory would be too high and the proximity almost assures that your neighbor is in the same predicament or soon going to be and a win gets you nothing but more mouths to feed unless of course you totally annihilate your enemy before they do the same to you.

The previous scenario has been playing out in Central Africa for some time and has now spread to the agriculturally poorer countries of the Middle East. Oil has saved some but theirs is but a temporary respite from the inevitable. Migration has mitigated the loss of life the upshot being that the migrants are bringing the problem with them and that is overpopulation. It is a cancer that has no cure but because of his greed, man has refused to acknowledge that although it is ultimately life threatening is not willing to take the steps to defer it.

The United States achieved its real economic apogee by the mid-1980s. We are already bankrupt but because we are our own creditor we can bail ourselves out by borrowing more money because nearly the entire world except the Chinese and India are in the dollar economy and only we and a few other countries still produce enough agricultural wealth to feed our population. Depending on how much you allow for each individual in kcal and the projected number of the U.S. population that critical point could be less than 50 years away. Yes, well within the lifetime of our grandchildren. If the exodus from Latin America, Africa and the Middle East accelerates that may be optimistic. Thousands of years of history and wars have demonstrated that those who determine the distribution of nature's wealth are either oblivious to the consequences of overpopulation or, if they are aware, believe they will be unaffected by it.

China has made a vain but unsuccessful attempt to stem its population. Other countries have not even tried. Projections by the United Nations, based on past data are probably overly pessimistic in order to try and get more attention paid to the problem but reality should have been enough. Thinking beyond our lifetime or several lifetimes has not been our strong suit. Perhaps it is because the inevitable has been dismissed as a possibility because many religions believe that before such an event happens a final judgement day will see us all in paradise or purgatory as the case may be. Whether this is true or not, man will have exhausted nature's resources and no science will be able to replace them, including the nutrients plants need to reproduce.

14

THE ULTIMATE RESULT

The earth has passed through over 10,000 years of human history, recorded or otherwise. Not in all those years has history recorded the implementation of a republican free market economy, the reason being that power, once acquired, is loath to its relinquishment. Even if such a system were implemented the inevitable is that eventually earth's resources necessary to produce and sustain life will reduce to zero. The only variable to this equation is time.

We have already reached the point where agricultural production is no longer keeping pace with the growth in population resulting in massive migrations and in some areas the consequences of dire shortages leading to starvation. Population increases are causing the irreversible conversion of nature's non-renewable resources into garbage and toxic wastes. The ultimate demise of the human race will come with the deaths of one society at a time. America has seen its halcyon days and China has already overtaken us as the world's leading economic power but, it too is in a more precarious balance than many of its neighbors and the United States. Who is next is anyone's guess because all of the previous societies are dying out or being mongrelized into mediocrity.

To pursue further in an attempt to outline the implementation of a system that will never see the light of day is not only foolhardy but insane.

12

THE ULTIMATE RESULT

Milton Keynes UK
Ingram Content Group UK Ltd.
UKHW040750020224
437154UK00001B/93